PRINCETON

ROBERT GAMBEE

W. W. Norton & Company
New York • London

For James F. Lawrence

Library of Congress Cataloging in Publication Data
Gambee, Robert
    Princeton
    Bibliography: p.
    Includes index.
    1. Princeton, N.J.   —Description—Views.
                            —History
                            —Schools
                            —Research Centers
    2. Lawrenceville, N.J. —Description—Views
                            —History, Lawrenceville School
    3. Princeton University
LD4611.G35 1987   378.749'67   86-21652
ISBN 0-393-02423-7
ISBN 0-393-30433-7

Printed in Japan by Dai Nippon Printing Company Ltd.

Designed by Jacqueline Schuman

Frontispiece: Canoeing on Lake Carnegie. This lake was
a gift to Princeton by Andrew Carnegie in 1906 and
always reminded him of a loch in his native Scotland.

The main entrance to Princeton today, along Washington Road under a canopy of hundred-year-old elm trees. The university initially occupied ten acres of land on Nassau Street. Today its holdings aggregate approximately 4000 acres including 2100 acres at the Forrestal Campus and Center.

Special Acknowledgements

For overall support of this project
Donald B. Brant, Jr.
Donald C. Broderick
John B. Fraser
John W. James
Charles A. Moran
Starling R. Lawrence
Robert H. Wadsworth
Van Zandt Williams, Jr.

For generous contributions of
time and knowledge for caption information
Lisa Cziffra
Nancy B. Eills
George B. Eager
Alexander Leitch
Samuel A. Schreiner, Jr.

For photographic and production assistance
Peter C. Bunnell
Bruce Campbell
Peter H. Grant
and especially
Tsuguo Tada

For administrative and marketing assistance
Louise Bachelder
Richard A. Cleaver
Elliott L. Gerlach
Mary M. Parks
José Pincay-Delgado

Contents

The Princeton-Kingston Bridge over the Millstone River. This bridge was built in the early 1790s and until recently handled all traffic entering Princeton from the East. The curve across the top of the photograph, reflected in the water at the bottom, is one of the arches of the old grist mill, built in 1755 by Jacob Skillman on the falls of the Millstone River.

INTRODUCTION
Princeton: Then and Now

A little over a century ago a historian of Princeton, John Hageman, wrote:

> *The notoriety which Princeton has acquired is not traceable to any peculiar advantages nature has bestowed on her, though her situation and embellishments make her an attractive place. But she is notable because, and only because, she has been the theatre of important public, historic events; and has been, and is, the seat of important public institutions…drawing around them from generation to generation distinguished public men and scholars…and sending forth from them, yearly, bands of trained young men to bless the world.*

In Hageman's time, "notoriety" meant fame and favorable recognition, not disrepute, while the adjective "public" referred to the well-being of the nation or the community at large, not merely the works of government. With those terms understood, the paragraph is not a bad characterization of today's Princeton—except that the "men" whom Princeton exports "to bless the world" now also include women.

Of course, when Hageman wrote, the College of New Jersey had not yet become Princeton University, a transition that officially occurred in 1896; nor did teaching and scholarship in the institution yet approach in range and influence what is now carried on there every day. Likewise, to the "important public institutions" that Hagemen knew—most notably the college, the theological seminary, the First Presbyterian Church and the Friends' Meetinghouse (both of the latter pre-Revolutionary establishments)—the subsequent years have seen added the world-renowned Institute for Advanced Study, the pioneering Educational Testing Service, whose outreach today is global, the nation's leading choir college, and the country's seventh most active performing arts center, not to mention several excellent secondary schools. Moreover, research centers, training facilities and other installations of more than fifty major corporations today claim rightful place among Princeton's more important "public institutions" in Hageman's sense of that term.

To be sure, the university remains the preeminent institution, largest employer, and brightest star in the Princeton constellation. With a relatively small student body, by American standards—roughly 6,000—its deliberate decisions to concentrate resources for qualitative performance rather than quantitative expansion have proved their worth. By any measure Princeton ranks among the world's leading research universities in those disciplines it has chosen to emphasize.

Despite necessarily high tuition charges—offset in part by scholarships provided by generous alumni donations and earlier endowments—it selects its students regardless of race, sex, or financial capability from among the brightest, most purposeful, and most promising applicants the nation has to offer. Under a faculty of active teacher-scholars, many world-renowned, a solid, balanced, individually challenging educational experience in the liberal arts is held out to every undergraduate student, not just to a few seeking honors. Meanwhile in graduate education and research, the quest for deeper insights and more comprehensive understanding goes on relentlessly. At the same time and in many ways, intellectual and cultural activities within the university keep spilling over to meet interests in the larger Princeton community and invite participation from it. There, as already suggested, the university now occupies at most the status of *primus inter pares* among Princeton's institutions of public importance where once it was largely dominant.

The historical origins of this now diverse, potent, yet unpretentious Princeton community are obscure, but by 1753 some of its citizens were well enough established and sufficiently enlightened to put up the £1,000 in cash, ten acres of cleared land, and two hundred acres of woodland required by the trustees of the College of New Jersey. This secured its removal from Newark to Princeton and in the process preempted the bid of rival New Brunswick. Undoubtedly expectations of increased trade and enhanced property values worked alongside appreciation of higher education as such to spur those early Princetonians on.

Provider of two signers of the Declaration of Independence, Richard Stockton and John Witherspoon—the latter also a leading proponent of the Revolutionary cause—and later of two presidents of the United States (James Madison and Woodrow Wilson), plus innumerable senators, representatives, justices of high courts, governors, and other notable public servants; site of a critical American victory in the Revolutionary War (January, 1777) and later meeting place of the Continental Congress (1783); home more recently of such departed luminaries as Grover Cleveland, Albert Einstein, Joseph Henry, Thomas Mann, Roger Sessions, Paul Tulane, and many others who have made a name in public affairs, education, science, the arts, and business: Princeton as a "theatre of important public, historic events" presents far too lengthy a chronicle for recounting here.

Suffice it that artful human embellishment in the forms of architecture and landscaping—coupled in recent times with fairly strict zoning regulations in the two Princeton municipalities—has created and sustained a gracious, open, easy ambience in what may be called Princeton proper. Lovely campuses disguise from outsiders the energetic intellectual ferment and the hard, long, demanding study that occupy Princeton's scholars. More deliberately deceptive architectural reconstruction, carried out during the Great Depression of the thirties, creates in the center of the borough the illusion of Georgian grace and self-confidence. Somehow a prevalent social style has been set that discourages ostentation, and if the informality nourished tends to be decorous, it is nonetheless genuine. Captains of leading industries, distinguished public servants, technological pathfinders, creative writers, scholars of world repute move about and mingle inconspicuously. In Princeton, it has been said with only slight hyperbole, a great many people are famous for something and hardly anyone makes a fuss about it.

But may the very ease and grace of life in Princeton now be coming to mean that Princeton is too seductive for its own good? Increasingly the two municipalities so named, which along with the university comprise its heart, are hard pressed to absorb those whom they draw in magnet-like because of the sheer visual charm, the stimulating human company, and the intellectual and cultural riches to be found within them. The prestige of a Princeton address, the convenient access to New York City and four international airports (two within a fifty-minute drive), the increasing dispersal of America's business activities out from the cities into formerly open areas, like central New Jersey—all these further pulls and pushes compound the problem, threatening the composition and character of "the old Princeton" and the services its municipalities can provide.

To any longtime resident, "Princeton" means the university and the two municipalities that surround it, Princeton Borough and Princeton Township, the former curled within the latter and nestled around the university. But the cluster of zip codes entitled to the Princeton, N.J., address reaches out to encompass nearly a dozen municipalities and altogether an area of a hundred square miles. Consequently far outside Princeton proper, especially to the east along Route One, one now finds new office buildings, research parks, and motels bearing the Princeton name.

Largely uncontrolled growth in these environs, in this new "greater Princeton" as it were, injects many new shoppers and sightseers into the historic center, while within it luxury shops catering to the new clientele crowd out long-held family stores. Real estate values and rental costs skyrocket, so that all too often children of long established Princeton families no longer can hope to live here, while less than affluent newcomers cannot expect to buy into the old Princeton unless a company bankrolls them. Meanwhile, traffic congestion grows steadily more dense and aggravating as development of the environs proceeds at breakneck speed.

What, then, Princeton will be as an area for living a decade or two hence, no one can say with certainty. One need not, however, despair about the community's ability to absorb and tame in time the heightened pressures that now bear on it. In any event, for most of Princeton's residents life now goes on much as before. Exurban informality interlaces easily with cosmopolitan diversity. The institutions that have made Princeton notable continue to pursue their historic functions with vigor and imagination. The embellished beauty of the place—especially in its trees and shrubs and lawns—persists. In Princeton there is much more that makes for a life that is at once pleasant and of "public" benefit than in many another place. This, I believe, will long be so.

Robert F. Goheen

Princeton is located midway between Philadelphia and New York, as this sign on the Stony Brook bridge indicates. The bridge was built in 1792 and is in active use today for most of the traffic entering Princeton from the West.

The History
of Princeton

With respect to situation, convenience and pleasure I do not know a more agreeable spot in America.

Charles Thompson, Secretary of the Continental Congress
June 30, 1783

These words were written by the Secretary of the Continental Congress to his wife after they had adjourned to Princeton from Philadelphia. By most accounts the adjournment was hurried because the war had just ended and word was spreading quickly among the American soldiers that Congress did not have enough funds to pay their wages. Fearing a mutiny, members of Congress thought it best to relocate for the time being and agreed to Elias Boudinot's suggestion to move to Princeton. The town was midway between the colonies' two major cities, Philadelphia and New York. It also had the distinction of being home to the College of New Jersey whose major building, Nassau Hall, was the largest structure in the country. The safe haven and tranquillity provided by the village of Princeton enabled the Congress to focus on the termination of the war period and on to the future of the newly formed United States of America.

Princeton had already played a significant role just six years earlier when General Washington quietly carried out an endplay around Lord Cornwallis one January night, cut off his supply column and won the first major victory for the Americans since the war began. Some historians believe this was the turning point of the war. Certainly it lifted the morale of the troops, and the Battle of Princeton is well documented in the lesson books on military strategy.

Although the town of Princeton was settled in the late 1600s its name was not adopted until 1724. The town was named in honor of William III, King of England and Prince of Orange-Nassau. The original settlement was called, and located on, Stony Brook. Most of the land had been purchased earlier by William Penn as part of an overall plan to secure the entire area between the Hudson and Delaware Rivers for Quakers. Penn later decided to devote his interests to Pennsylvania. By 1695 Richard Stockton, a Quaker, Daniel Brinson, Benjamin Clarke, and William Olden had all purchased properties between Stony Brook and the Millstone River. Two years later Benjamin FitzRandolph purchased 316 acres between what are now Alexander Street and Washington Road, land that later formed the original site of the College of New

The pastoral nature of Princeton is reflected in the graceful stone arches of the Stony Brook bridge (*above*) and the green meadows of a dairy farm (*opposite*). Princeton was originally settled in the late 1600s and was officially named Princeton in 1724 following two communities to the north, Kingston and Queenston. Much of the fertile soil surrounding the community is still used for agricultural purposes such as nurseries, sod farms, and dairy and produce farms.

Jersey. The lots of the early settlers were long and narrow enabling each to have both meadows and stream. Agriculture—farming as well as livestock—was the only occupation, and its heritage still continues in the Princeton community today (although under significant pressure from the real estate developers). The first industry came to the area in 1715 when Thomas Potts built two grist mills and a bolting mill at Stony Brook, the remains of which are still visible today at the edge of the Stony Brook bridge. The remains of another mill may be seen near the Kingston bridge.

The earliest surviving structure is "The Barracks," part of the original Richard Stockton house built out of native field stone around 1696 near to the "overland trail" (now Nassau and Stockton Streets). Most of the early houses were simple and utilitarian. There was no formal style, indeed there was not even a uniformity among them since the settlers had arrived from different parts of the colonies and lacked a cohesive background.

As the farm economy developed, the original style of the dwellings was expanded and by the mid-1700s yeoman farmhouses were evolving into manor houses. Some of the landowners began adding "Esquire" to their names. Richard and Annis Stockton set the new pace in the third quarter of the eighteenth century with the construction of "Morven," a beautiful example of the new Georgian style that was evolving in the colonies. Georgian architecture derives from the late sixteenth-century Italian architect Palladio, and was popularized in England in the mid-1600s by Christopher Wren. Georgian architecture started to become popular in America in the early 1700s, one of the finest early examples being the Governor's Palace in Williamsburg.

A concern for pure form, symmetry, and amplitude in the living areas is characteristic of "Morven" and the other Georgian manor houses that were being constructed in Princeton in the second half of the eighteenth century: "Tusculum," "Mansgrove," and the reconstructions to "Castle Howard" and "Maybury Hill."

At the same time that Princeton was helping itself to grow in esteem, the College of New Jersey, which had been operating in the home of Jonathan Dickinson in Elizabeth, was looking for a new location. The college had been chartered in 1746 by Governor John Hamilton, at the request of members of the Presbyterian congregations. It must be remembered that all of the colonies' new colleges were founded by religious groups in order to provide ministers for the new settlers: Harvard and Yale were founded Congregationalists (Yale originally being called the Collegiate School), William & Mary and Columbia (originally Kings College) by Anglicans, Rutgers (Queens College) by Dutch Reformed, and Brown by the Baptists. The secularization of the colleges did not occur until the early 1800s.

While both New Brunswick and Elizabeth were vying for the location of the college, the Philadelphia synod thought a location more equidistant between New York and Philadelphia might be sought. The college then considered New Brunswick and Princeton as final possibilities, and it stipulated that the community where it would locate must provide ten acres of cleared land, two hundred acres of woodlands for fuel, and £1000 in New Jersey currency. A group of citizens of Princeton, under the leadership of William FitzRandolph and John Sergeant, announced suddenly at the college's trustee meeting in January, 1753, that they had met the requirements, and the town was selected. Construction of a new building began the following year and upon completion in 1756 was the largest in the colonies. Governor Jonathan Belcher mercifully declined the suggestion that it be named for him and suggested it be named instead for the King, William III, Prince of Orange-Nassau.

From the first meeting in 1753 to the present, the town and university have grown together, each benefiting from the presence of the other and the combination seeming to attract additional educational and research institutions to the area. Boston may boast of more schools and California of more university campuses, but Princeton is blessed with more leading institutions woven into a fabric more inspiring and peaceful than most other locations in the country. Mark Twain once said, "Princeton would suit me as well as Heaven, better in fact, for I shouldn't care for that society up there." Many others have written about the town over the years, commenting on its unique characteristics, but the words of one famous resident are among the most touching:

I am almost ashamed to be living in such peace while all the rest struggle and suffer. But after all, it is still best to concern oneself with eternals, for from them alone flows that spirit that can restore peace and serenity to the world of humans.

Albert Einstein
1936

It is quiet now on the Princeton battlefield. But in early 1777 Washington gained a strategic victory over Lord Cornwallis that may have been the turning point in the Revolutionary War.

Cornwallis had been marching through New Jersey determined at long last to crunch Washington ("the Fox") and his rebels. The Americans retreated slowly to Trenton. On a cold January 2d evening Cornwallis stopped short of the Americans' camp. The latter were poor, ill-equipped and had dug in for the night. The thud and scrape of picks and shovels could be overheard by the British sentinels on the other side of the creek and indicated the Americans were strengthening their camp against a morning attack. But by daybreak,

the Americans had vanished—not a gun or soldier remained. Their position was abandoned, and while Cornwallis was having morning tea, Washington and his troops were attacking the British from behind. The Battle of Princeton has long been studied as the classic example of how a general whose forces were hopelessly outnumbered surprised his opposition by marching around and attacking from the rear. Washington pushed ahead and recaptured Nassau Hall later that day. This was the Americans' first major victory in the war, and the boost in the troops' morale helped them to fight on to a successful conclusion six years later.

The Thomas Clarke House (*ca.* 1770). In 1770 Thomas Clarke, a Quaker farmer, acquired this land which had been owned by the Clarke family since 1696.

This white clapboard, two-story home contains six rooms including the main keeping room with its massive fireplace, butterfly cupboard and handsome birdcage Windsor chairs. At the far end of the keeping room table (*opposite, bottom*) is a sugar loaf, standing upright to the left of the candlesticks. This is made of refined sugar, imported from Cuba. Sugar loaves were either ground up or used in chunks. Upstairs there are two bedrooms and a spinning room. Note the bed warmer next to the fireplace in the upstairs bedroom (*opposite, top*), a common device to warm the sheets with hot coals on winter nights.

General Hugh Mercer led a successful encounter with the British troops in Clarke's fields and, when joined by the main American column, managed to rout the British. The Americans went on to recapture the town of Princeton, and with this reinforcement Washington went on to gain control of most of New Jersey. Mercer unfortunately died in the Clarke homestead of battle wounds.

"Rockingham" (*ca.* 1710, 1764). While the Continental Congress met in Princeton in 1783, this homestead was rented from the widow of Judge John Berrien as the headquarters for George Washington. John Berrien had become Justice of the New Jersey Supreme Court in 1764.

The original parts of this house, built by John Harrison, show a strong resemblance to early Connecticut homes, especially the gunstock corner posts. These are flared at the top to carry the weight of the structural beams. In the room used by Washington's aides (*opposite, top*) is a trundle bed. These were commonly used at the time in order to save space. In the main bedroom (*opposite, below*) are a handsome New Jersey wing chair and New England tea table. The house is located north of Princeton in the community of Rocky Hill.

Opposite: The Prayer Room of Nassau Hall. After the Revolutionary War, the Continental Congress fled to Princeton from Philadelphia to escape a possible mutiny of the American troops over wages it was unable to pay. Nassau Hall was the largest building in the colonies and during 1783 served as the capital of the new United States. During this time the trustees of the College of New Jersey persuaded Washington to sit for a portrait by Charles Willson Peale, one of the few of him ever painted from a live sitting (*above*).

The other portraits are of William Paterson (*opposite*, *right*) and James Madison (*opposite*, *left*), alumni of the college (1763 and 1771, respectively). Paterson was head of the New Jersey delegation to the constitutional convention, associate justice of the United States Supreme Court, and a trustee of the college. At the constitutional convention, he offered the New Jersey "small states" plan based on population in opposition to Madison's "large states" plan with two representatives per state. Ultimately a compromise supported by Oliver Ellsworth, another alumnus, was adopted.

Madison, considered by many to be the "father of the Constitution," sponsored the Bill of Rights in the 1790s and went on to be secretary of state and the fourth president of the United States, guiding the country through a second war for independence with Great Britain. He was the first president of the alumni association and, with Thomas Jefferson, was a co-founder of the University of Virginia.

Nos. 498, 487 and 481 Stockton Street. These three pre-Revolutionary homes on Stockton Street are located in the original settlement of Stony Brook. The land was first acquired by William Penn in 1682 and sold to Richard Stockton in 1693. The brook provided necessary water for the households and their livestock until wells could be dug. There was also a grist mill operated by the Quakers and powered by the brook. No. 487 (*opposite, above*) is probably the earliest of these houses and is of an unusual three-story design. The stones came from the land as it was cleared. The foundation for the barn of No. 487 is now used by the clapboard house next door at No. 481 (*opposite, bottom*).

The land for the Quaker Meetinghouse is believed to have been given by the Clarke family, who built the house at No. 498. This house has an eight-foot-wide fireplace on the ground floor where the original kitchen was located (*above*).

27

Opposite: "The Barracks" (1696), 32 Edgehill Street, built by Richard Stockton. The Stocktons came from Long Island and were drawn by the prospect of developing the rich farmland in central New Jersey. The earliest section of "The Barracks" was built in 1696 and is thus the oldest house in Princeton. Richard Stockton willed the house to his son John, whose own son, also Richard, was a signer of the Declaration of Independence and lived at "Morven."

From 1689 to 1763, the United Kingdom and France had frequent skirmishes in America for control of the territory, these being known as the French and Indian Wars. By the mid-1700s the people of Princeton had tired of having to provide housing for the British troops. A petition was submitted to the king that residences be purchased or rented for the sole purpose of quartering the troops. In the 1760s the house left the Stockton family. Thomas Lawrence was one of its subsequent owners and is believed to have quartered Alexander Hamilton, the New York delegate, when Congress met in Princeton. The Springdale Farm, which included "The Barracks," returned to the Stockton family in the early nineteenth century.

Above: The Quaker Meetinghouse (*ca.* 1759), replacing an earlier wooden structure built in 1724. The same warm yellowish sandstone used in Nassau Hall was used here three years later, probably by the same mason. The Quakers settled along Stony Brook beginning in the 1680s. During the Battle of Princeton this meetinghouse was a hospital for the troops.

"Morven" (*ca.* 1755, 1848), 55 Stockton Street, built by Richard Stockton, a signer of the Declaration of Independence, and named after the mythical home of Fingal in *The Poems of Ossian*. It is one of the first expressions of elegance and sophistication in the colonies. The Georgian style, highly rational and formal, expressed the mind of the Age of Enlightenment, in which man was thought to be no longer subject to the whims of God and Nature and in which he was felt capable of bringing a high measure of order to society. The house has been added to many times.

The ground plan called for symmetry and amplitude, with an impressive entrance hallway leading from the main door to the garden door on the opposite side. This also allowed privacy to the rooms flanking the hall. "Morven" was considered the grandest of Princeton's country houses and became for many years the home of the governor of New Jersey.

Richard Stockton was in the first graduating class of the College of New Jersey (1748), went abroad in 1767 at the request of the trustees to invite John Witherspoon to become president of the college, and was a delegate to the Continental Congress in 1776. During the Revolution, Annis Stockton buried the family silver in the garden in order to keep it from being stolen and melted down. After the war, her brother, Elias Boudinot, stayed here when he was president of the Continental Congress, and the combined Boudinot-Stockton household was lavish in dispensing hospitality to visiting congressmen and their families.

"Maybury Hill" (*ca.* 1735, 1768) (*above*), "Mansgrove" (1730, 1800) (*opposite, top*), and "Castle Howard" (*ca.* 1760, 1842) (*opposite, bottom*).

None of the other Georgian farmhouses in Princeton were conceived on a scale as grand as "Morven." Nevertheless, these three gracious homes reflect a continuing departure from the smaller, more utilitarian houses. All three have been expanded afterwards.

"Maybury Hill" was built on Snowden Lane by Aaron Hewes, whose son, Joseph Hewes, was born here and later became a signer of the Declaration of Independence from North Carolina. Other Princeton signers included his brother-in-law, Richard Stockton,

Dr. Benjamin Rush, and John Witherspoon.

"Mansgrove" was built near the Mt. Lucas Road by Judge Thomas Leonard and his wife Susanna Stockton in the early eighteenth century.

The earliest section of "Castle Howard" was laid out in the early 1700s on the Princeton-Kingston Road, making it, along with "The Barracks," one of the oldest structures in Princeton. The land may have been part of Richard Stockton's original purchase. The main section of the house was built about 1760. In 1763 it was purchased by Capt. William Howard of His Majesty's 17th Regiment, from whom it derives the name.

Opposite, *top*: the Gulick-Hodge-Scott House (*ca.* 1746, 1810) on Herrontown Road. The western wing of this house (at the left in the photograph) has the low ceilings and enormous central fireplace and bake oven characteristic of pre-Revolutionary homes. The elegant brick section is more Georgian and shows a greater consciousness of aesthetic values. It dates from 1810.

Above: "Tusculum" (1773) on Cherry Hill Road was built by John Witherspoon, sixth president of the College of New Jersey. Witherspoon came from Scotland in 1768 and was a signer of the Declaration of Independence. He was instrumental in increasing both the enrollment and endowment of the college, putting it on a sound financial basis and assuring its success as a viable educational institution. "Tusculum" is of a simple country Georgian style. It is named for an ancient Roman summer resort where nobles had summer villas. *Opposite*, *bottom*: The handsome stone barn was built about 1815.

Above: Beatty House, 19 Vandeventer Avenue, built by Colonel Jacob Hyer *ca*. 1780. Colonel Erkuries Beatty purchased the house in 1816 and expanded it. The Marquis de Lafayette stayed here in 1825 (Beatty was a former aide). The house originally stood, during the Revolutionary War, on Nassau Street where the university's Firestone Library is presently located.

Opposite, top: A pre-Revolutionary home at 325 Nassau St. (*ca*. 1750).

Opposite, bottom: "Queen's Court," 341 Nassau St., built by John Harrison *ca*. 1790, 1805 and presently the headquarters for the architect Michael Graves. The name comes from the affectionate reference by Princeton students to a girls' preparatory school housed here in the late nineteenth century. The girls were preparing for Evelyn College, which was established in 1887 to become the female adjunct to Princeton University but which eventually succumbed in 1897 from lack of financial support.

This area, at the intersection of Nassau and Harrison Streets, was originally called "Queenston" (between Kingston and Princeton) and later "Jugtown" after a pottery that operated between 1760 and 1860. The Jugtown well was a popular meeting spot until it was closed over in 1932. Before the time of strenuous athletics, the seminarians would walk after their afternoon prayers from the seminary to Jugtown and back.

Opposite, top: No. 298 Nassau Street (*ca.* 1830), possibly designed by Charles Steadman.

Opposite, below: No. 342 Nassau Street (*ca.* 1730). *Below*: 159 Nassau Street (*ca.* 1763). These houses are tall and narrow, characteristic of the style of the time. During the stay of the Continental Congress, Mrs. Scott had No. 342 listed as a bed and breakfast stop, and later, during the Civil War, it was a stop on the "Underground Railway."

Left: No. 274 Nassau Street (*ca.* 1820). Note the unusual triangular lintels over the windows and the delicate portico.

The Joseph Henry House (1837) on Nassau Street. Joseph Henry was the leading American scientist after Benjamin Franklin. In fact, he was perhaps the only American research physicist of his time. He was a professor of natural philosophy (i.e., physics) at the college from 1832 to 1846, designed and built this house for himself, and made significant scientific contributions in the field of electromagnetism. He built the largest electromagnet in the world, discovered the principle of self inductance in the flow of electric current, and assisted Samuel Morse in the invention of the telegraph. In fact, he practiced the telegraph code by sending signals on wires he had strung from his office to the house indicating when he would be home for lunch. In 1846, Professor Henry left to become the first secretary of the Smithsonian Institution. Since 1973, this house has been the official residence of the dean of the university faculty.

Maclean House (1756), finished in the same year as Nassau Hall, was designed and built by Robert Smith. Until "Prospect" was acquired in 1878, this was the official residence of the college's presidents and later its deans of the faculty. In 1968 it became the home of the Alumni Council and was named in honor of John Maclean, 1816, founder of the Alumni Association and member of the faculty for fifty years, rising from tutor to president. He held the college together during the challenges of the devastating fire in Nassau Hall in 1855 and the loss of a third of the student enrollment during the Civil War. John Maclean's father was the college's first professor of chemistry in 1795 and his experiments were probably the first made in any American college.

Opposite: This eighteenth-century room in Firestone Library contains John Witherspoon's personal collection of books as well as his slant-top writing desk. Above the desk is a portrait of Jonathan Belcher, governor of the Province of New Jersey when the college was founded. It was Belcher who suggested naming Nassau Hall after King William III, Prince of Orange-Nassau.

Above: Sunday morning on Nassau Street. On the right is Bainbridge House, 158 Nassau Street, built *ca.* 1765 by Job Stockton and presently the headquarters of the Historical Society of Princeton.

The interior of Bainbridge House. In 1776 it was used as a headquarters by the British and in 1783 it housed members of the Continental Congress. During 1774, when Robert Stockton owned the house, it was being rented to Dr. Absalom Bainbridge, whose son, William Bainbridge, later commander of the U.S.S. *Constitution*, was born here. From 1911 to 1966 this building was the Princeton Public Library.

These furnishings are from the Boudinot collection of Princeton University. Elias Boudinot was a member of the Continental Congress and was elected its president in 1782. He held this office during the 1783 Nassau Hall session and lived at "Morven" with his sister and brother-in-law, Annis and Richard Stockton. Boudinot is best remembered for initiating the Congressional resolution that led to establishing Thanksgiving a national holiday in 1789. He was also a trustee of the college for forty-nine years.

The Historical Society of Princeton was founded in 1938 and presently occupies the house. Its aims are to encourage interest and promote research and education in local history and culture through exhibitions, talks, tours and publications.

Above: The Presbyterian Church of Lawrenceville. The congregation of this church was established in 1698 and is one of the oldest in the country. The front part of the present church building was constructed in 1764 and enlarged in 1835.

Opposite: The Theophilus Phillips House (1750, 1790). Phillips was the son of an original settler from Long Island, became a judge of the county courts and resigned in 1752 to set up a public house. His grandson added the larger main section of the house.

Lawrenceville

The town of Lawrenceville, first settled in 1690, was organized in 1696 under the name "Maidenhead" after a town on the Thames in England. Only in 1816 was it renamed after Captain John Lawrence ("Don't give up the ship"), a New Jersey naval hero during the War of 1812. He was the commander of the *Chesapeake* and was mortally wounded in a battle with the British in 1813.

The first purchasers of land were John Brearley, Richard Ridgeway, Mary Davis, and Thomas Green—all in 1690. By 1694, settlers began to arrive from Newtown, the name the English had given to the early Dutch settlement in Brooklyn. Travel was by horse and pack animals. There were no trails wide enough for wagons but fortunately the Indians were friendly. The congregation in Maidenhead was among the first organized in the area. The town was on the trade route between New Brunswick and Trenton and became the largest settlement in the county. Mary McCauley, better known as "Molly Pitcher" for her heroism in carrying water to American soldiers during the battle of Monmouth (June 28, 1778), was born here. Many years later, in 1810, Dr. Isaac Brown founded his Classical and Commercial High School for boys, now known as the Lawrenceville School.

Today, the township of Lawrenceville covers approximately twenty square miles and contains about 23,000 inhabitants.

The Ralph Hunt House (1706), also known as "Old Brick" (*above*), the John Brearley House (*ca.* 1690) (*opposite, top*), and the John Dagworthy House (1720), also known as "Cherry Grove" (*opposite, bottom*). These are the three oldest homes in Lawrenceville. John Brearley was one of the original settlers in Lawrenceville and became well established in the community before Ralph Hunt arrived in 1694. Hunt's house has had many uses over the years—as a farmhouse, a school infirmary for contagious diseases, a residence for school instructors, a student dormitory, and a home for the Lawrenceville School librarian. Note the similarity in design to "The Barracks," Princeton's oldest house.

"Cherry Grove," built in 1720, was purchased by John Sergeant in 1756. In 1751 he proposed the site in Princeton ultimately chosen in 1753 by the College of New Jersey as its future home. He was active in its founding and was its treasurer from 1750 to 1776. In 1770, Sergeant sold "Cherry Grove" to his nephew George Green, whose son Richard Green helped organize the Lawrenceville School.

Opposite, top: The William Phillips House (*ca.* 1734). This house was originally a tavern and is one of the oldest in the area. Its cellar has an unusual beehive bake-oven that is over five feet in diameter. The interior doors of the house are of solid cherry, and the largest of the outbuildings, a smokehouse, still retains the aroma of smoked hams.

Opposite, bottom: The Richard Montgomery Green House (1815). Richard Green built his house with stone from the Cherry Grove quarry and named it "Harmony Hall." It remained in the Green family for four generations and after a period of interval owners was acquired by the Lawrenceville School for a master's res-

idence. Richard and Charles Green were among the school's first seven trustees.

Above: The Samuel Hunt House. (*ca.* 1760) Samuel Hunt was a brother of Ralph Hunt and along with Theophilus Phillips arrived in Maidenhead around 1694 from Newtown (Brooklyn). The house has eight fireplaces, including one that is eight and a half feet long. In the attic is an unusual chamber that was used as a smokehouse, with a flue leading into the chimney. The windows are held in position by springs in the sashes, notched to hold the window at a given opening. The stone probably came from the Cherry Grove quarry.

51

Nineteenth-century Princeton

The prosperity of the nation as a whole, combined with the opening of the Delaware and Raritan Canal and the Camden and Amboy Railroad in the 1830s, brought substantial new construction to Princeton. One individual, an architect by the name of Charles Steadman, who already had been working as a carpenter on the First Presbyterian Church in 1820, had a greater influence on Princeton architecture than anyone else. The Greek Revival style (with Roman details) was spreading throughout the country, influenced largely by Thomas Jefferson. On these and the following pages are shown the major architectural accomplishments of Charles Steadman and John Notman.

Opposite, top: Charles Steadman built a series of Greek Revival houses on Alexander Street when the new road was opened up in 1832. It was originally called Canal Street and later renamed in honor of Rev. Archibald Alexander, the first professor of the seminary. The houses represent Princeton's earliest and best example of cohesive urban design.

Opposite, below: The Princeton Battle Monument, the result of seventy-five years of effort and the energies of Allan Marquand and Bayard Stockton. It was designed by Thomas Hastings, sculpted by Frederick MacMonnies, and unveiled in 1922 by President Warren Harding. It depicts Washington on horseback sternly refusing defeat at the Battle of Princeton and inspiring his troops to final victory. On the back is the following inscription, written by Dean West of the graduate school:

> *Here memory lingers*
> *to recall*
> *the guiding mind*
> *whose daring plan*
> *outflanked the foe*
> *and turned dismay to hope*
> *when Washington*
> *with swift resolve*
> *marched through the night*
> *to fight at dawn*
> *and venture all*
> *in one victorious battle*
> *for our freedom.*

Homes of two prominent Princetonians: Einstein House (*opposite, top*), 112 Mercer Street, built around 1840 by Samuel Stevens. Albert Einstein lived here from 1935 until he died in 1955. Woodrow Wilson House (*above*), 72 Library Place, built in 1836 by Charles Steadman. The Woodrow Wilsons lived here beginning in 1890. This house is considered one of Steadman's finest. Pleasing proportions plus unusually fine details are used throughout with a freedom and vigor that delight the eye. It was originally called "The Ridge" after its first owner, John Breckinridge of the Princeton Theological Seminary.

Sheldon House (*opposite, bottom*), 10 Mercer Street (*ca.* 1840), was moved from Northampton, Mass. to New Bedford and then on a barge to Princeton in 1868. The Rev. George Sheldon was able to inherit the house only if he agreed to live in it. Since Massachusetts was not as agreeable as his Princeton environment at the time of the inheritance, he simply moved the house.

"Drumthwacket," 344 Stockton Street, built around 1835 for Charles Smith Olden, Governor of New Jersey, and greatly expanded in 1896. It was probably designed by Charles Steadman. The name means "Wooded Hill." For many years this was the home of Moses Taylor Pyne, one of Princeton University's most substantial benefactors and the one who fostered the development of its Collegiate Gothic style.

While Pyne lived at "Drumthwacket," it became the focus of much of the social life of the university and town. The grounds were always open to visitors, and many students spent pleasant hours strolling the paths through deer parks and woods to a series of small lakes and gardens. It supposedly took a staff of sixty to maintain. The State of New Jersey recently acquired "Drumthwacket" as a residence for its governor.

Princeton stands for so much that is important. Not only for intellectual enrichment but for the value of service and the importance of friendship.
　　　　　　　　　—Thomas H. Kean, Governor of New Jersey

Palmer House, One Bayard Lane, built in 1825 by Charles Steadman for Robert Stockton and his Charleston bride. The house is owned by the university and named for Edgar Palmer, class of 1903, who moved into it in 1923. He was a charter trustee and donor of Palmer Stadium in 1914. His greatest gift to the community was the tastefully designed Palmer Square, located down Nassau Street from his home.

Above: Walter Lowrie House, 83 Stockton Street, built in 1849 by John Notman for John Potter Stockton in the Italianate style. This was the first of a new style of house for Princeton, the villa. Others that followed were "Prospect" in 1852, "Guernsey Hall" in 1850, a remodeled "Drumthwacket" in 1896, Junius Morgan's "Constitution Hill" in 1897, and finally Archibald Russell's "Edgerstoune" in 1903. "Edgerstoune" is presently the home of the Hun School.

In 1860, Lowrie House became the home of Paul Tulane, a Princeton alumnus who founded Tulane University. In 1882, the College of New Jersey, already planning to change its name to Princeton University, turned down a munificent offer of money by Mr. Tulane because it would have required naming the col-

lege after him. Lowrie is named for its most recent owner who left it to the university in 1960 to be the official residence of its president.

Opposite, top: The Joseph Olden House, 130 Stockton Street, built *ca*. 1760 and "Gothicized" by John Notman in 1848 to blend in with Lowrie House and Allan Marquand's "Fieldwood" (Guernsey Hall).

Opposite, bottom: Prospect Gardens. Although smaller than those of Pyne's "Drumthwacket," these gardens, laid out by Mrs. Woodrow Wilson, are nevertheless the center of peaceful strolls by university students, faculty, and visitors. They are carefully maintained, and the university even manages to include orange tulips in the spring.

"Prospect" on the university's campus, built in 1852 by John Notman for John Potter. Potter was the son of a wealthy merchant from Charleston who built Palmer House for his daughter and her husband, Richard Stockton. "Prospect" is in the Italianate style favored by Notman and shows a complete break from the organized symmetry of the Georgian period. The house was given to the college in 1878 for use as a residence by President McCosh and his successors. McCosh considered it to be the finest college president's house in the world and said upon retiring and leaving it that he felt like Adam leaving Eden. Since Lowrie House became the university's official presidential residence in 1968, "Prospect" has been the home of its faculty club.

Above: The Nassau Club, 6 Mercer Street, originally built in 1814 as the home of Samuel Miller, one of the first professors of the Princeton Theological Seminary. In 1903, it was acquired by the Nassau Club under the presidency of Woodrow Wilson.

Opposite, top: The University Cottage Club, founded in 1886. This building was designed by McKim, Mead & White in 1904.

Opposite, bottom: Quadrangle Club, founded in 1901. The present building was designed by H.O. Milliken in 1916.

Opposite, top: Colonial Club, founded in 1891. The familiar, columned clubhouse was designed by F.G. Stuart in 1907.

Opposite, far left: Ivy Club, founded in 1879. Cope and Stewardson designed this facility in 1900.

Opposite, left: Charter Club, founded in 1901. This Georgian-style building was designed by Mellor and Meigs in 1914.

The Princeton eating clubs were first organized by the students in 1855 in order to provide adequate dining facilities for themselves. The refectory food had become so intolerable that the students had taken to a dramatic form of protest: at a given signal up would go the windows and out would fly the tablecloths with all that was on them. The eating clubs were not affiliated with the university but rather were, and remain today, private clubs. With the help of their own graduate members, they built the handsome brick and stone clubhouses on Prospect Street (or Avenue, as it is officially designated). By the turn of the century, two-thirds of the upperclassmen were members of eating clubs. It was Woodrow Wilson's concern for the remaining one-third who were not in the clubs that led him to promote his "quad" or residential-college plan, which is now being implemented.

Above: The Scribner Building (1911), 41 William Street, home of the Princeton University Press and a gift from Charles Scribner, class of 1875. The university press was founded in 1905 and is a separate, financially independent corporation with its own board of trustees. It publishes about 100 new titles each year for the university and other non-profit organizations. Also housed in the Scribner Building is the *Princeton Alumni Weekly*, founded in 1900 and presently printing more issues each year than any other alumni magazine in the United States.

Palmer Square, West, from the steps of the Nassau
Presbyterian Church.

The Town
of Princeton

There are twenty-seven communities in the United States named "Princeton" but the two originals are in New Jersey—Princeton Borough (the town), the smaller and older of the two, and Princeton Township which surrounds it. Together they have a population of about 26,000. The borough was incorporated on February 11, 1813 and the township was formed in 1838 with the creation of Mercer County.

Both the borough and the township are separate political entities with their own systems of municipal courts, elected officials, and police departments. Only one person has served as mayor of both the Borough and Township—B. Franklin ("Uncle Ben") Bunn, a beloved citizen of Princeton who had a finger in every pie for over sixty years. He was a founder and officer of the Princeton Savings and Loan Association and the Princeton Laundry, a director of the Princeton Water Company, and for thirty years president of the trustees of the First Presbyterian Church. He was a director of the United Fund, the Princeton Hospital, and the Chamber of Commerce, and a trustee of Westminster Choir College. He was manager of the University Store and the McCarter Theatre and graduate treasurer of the Triangle Club, the *Daily Princetonian*, and the *Princeton Tiger*. He was an official timer at the football, basketball, track, and swimming contests, and during his free time grew all of his own vegetables in his garden.

Princeton has been blessed with many fine citizens of similar note over the years—Moses Taylor Pyne, Edgar and Stephen Palmer, and Allan Marquand among the most prominent, and hundreds of others who have made significant contributions of time and talents to the community.

One of the most ambitious undertakings was the creation of Palmer Square in the mid-1930s by Edgar O. Palmer. The buildings were designed by Thomas Stapleton and represent one of the first major colonial restoration projects in the country after the restoration of Williamsburg by the Rockefeller family in the 1920s. The development of Palmer Square, including significant expansion of the Nassau Inn, is being continued today under the leadership of Arthur Collins as part of an $80 million development program. The tasteful evolution of Princeton at Palmer Square and along Nassau Street, enabling the town to expand into the twentieth century without any neon lights, for example, is a tribute to those concerned about preservation of its important heritage and maintenance of an atmosphere worthy of a major university's presence. The borough's new Historic Preservation Committee is formally overseeing this trend today. The Baltimore Dairy Lunch ("the Balt")—popular with students and truck drivers for generations because of its affordable cuisine and twenty-four hour service—has given way to other restaurants tastefully tucked into Tudor facades. Until recently, even the bus station was situated in a building of sixteenth-century English design.

When Samuel Davies returned from England in 1754 with contributions for the construction of Nassau Hall (a journey that took three months to cross the Atlantic, including a three-week layover in Plymouth due to bad weather), there was no other way to get to Princeton from New York than on horseback. Coach service had not started and the railroad was a hundred years in the future. Today the transportation system is somewhat more convenient. The main rail line from New York to Washington passed through the town until 1867, when the route was straightened and Princeton became connected by way of a shuttle called the PJ&B (Princeton Junction and Back, also known as "the Dinky"). Various interstate highways have greatly improved overload service from the days of my pre-turnpike youth when the trip from New York was a major event. Princeton even has its own airport now.

But Princeton is steadfastly proud of its past and is not anxious to part from it—a reassuring attitude in what has become a very disposable-oriented society. This is both the anchor and the inspiration that have enabled the community to evolve into a major research center and university town without losing the small, personal touch all of us, as individuals, seek to maintain.

Palmer Square, East, showing One Palmer Square and
the town's kiosk.

69

Above and opposite: Palmer Square. The buildings around the square were designed by Thomas Stapleton in 1936 at the request of Edgar Palmer, class of 1903, who conceived the idea and financed its development. Stapleton worked for one of the Rockefeller firms, and after the restoration of Colonial Williamsburg by the Rockefeller family in the 1920s, this is one of the oldest Colonial restoration and development projects in the country.

Above: the FitzRandolph Gateway of Princeton University, at the intersection of Witherspoon and Nassau Streets, built in 1905 and designed by McKim, Mead & White. The gateway is named for Nathaniel FitzRandolph who gave the land on which Nassau Hall stands. In the mid-seventeenth century, he, more than any other citizen of Princeton, was responsible for raising necessary funds and providing the land which enabled the College of New Jersey to relocate from New Brunswick.

Opposite: the Nassau Inn (also known as "the Nass") has been operating continually as an inn since 1757. It was moved to its present location in the center of Palmer Square and to a new building in 1937. Its name was officially changed from the Nassau Tavern to the Nassau Inn in 1960. With the completion of a new wing in 1985, the Inn has one hundred twenty-eight bedrooms plus extensive conference rooms. On spring Sundays, H. Gross & Co., one of the Square's new merchants, arranges croquet tournaments on the green.

Nassau Street, looking east (*above*) and west (*opposite, top*). This is the main thoroughfare of Princeton and appears on the earliest maps as the Kings Highway or the Post Road, part of the important road from New York to Philadelphia. Many people have traveled along it, including Paul Revere in December, 1773, on his way to Philadelphia with news of the Boston Tea Party.

Twentieth-century shops abound now but there are still no neon signs on Nassau Street.

Opposite, bottom: Nassau Christian Center, 1870, formerly known as St. Andrew's Presbyterian Church for a congregation organized in 1847. It was designed by Henry Leard.

The atmosphere of a university town is prevalent on Nassau Street. Lower Pyne (*opposite*) was a gift of Moses Taylor Pyne in 1896 and was designed by Raleigh Gildersleeve after sixteenth-century houses in Chester, England. Both Lower Pyne and its companion, Upper Pyne (razed in 1964) were designed for shops on the ground floor and dormitory rooms for students on the upper floors. The students loved the location, close to "the Balt" and Renwick's, both popular restaurants, as well as the movie theaters. The dormitory days ended in 1950. In 1985, the university sold Lower Pyne to British-owned Commonwealth Realty Trust, a real estate investment company whose headquarters are located here.

Above, left: The Arts Center of Princeton, 102 Witherspoon Street. The Arts Center was originally built in 1939 as the Witherspoon Community House by the U.S. Government's Works Progress Administration. It has subsequently been leased by the Borough of Princeton to the Arts Council. The Arts Council of Princeton was formed in 1967 to increase public awareness and participation in the arts. The Council operates the Center as a meeting place for individuals and corporations interested in the arts. It has dance studios, a theatre, classrooms, gallery space, a photographic laboratory and a bookstore. The Center has approximately twenty artists in residence, and three hundred twenty individual members belong to the Arts Council.

Above, right: The Gallup Organization, Inc. on Bank Street has its roots in The Gallup Poll, started in 1935 by Dr. George H. Gallup. The Gallup Poll was the first organization to utilize scientific procedures to measure the political, social and economic climate of America, and it has achieved a worldwide reputation for its accuracy in pre-election surveys. The Gallup Organization was established to serve the needs of business, government, foundations, associations and others wishing to apply survey research to problem solving. It employs over one hundred full-time professionals as well as over nine hundred part-time telephone and personal interviewers. It has affiliates in over forty nations with the capability of conducting survey research throughout the free world.

Opposite, top: Shops and Callery pear trees on Witherspoon Street. *Opposite, bottom*: The offices of the *Princeton Packet* on Witherspoon Street, one of the oldest newspapers in the country. John Witherspoon came from Scotland in 1768 to be the college's sixth president. He was a strong defender of the independence movement, a member of the Continental Congress, and he signed the Declaration of Independence against England.

The Nassau Presbyterian Church (*left*), designed by Thomas Walter in 1835, replacing earlier structures built in 1762 and 1813. Until Alexander Hall was built in 1892, most commencement exercises of the college were held in this church. The commencement of 1783 was particularly memorable because it was attended by George Washington and the entire Congress of the United States.

The congregation of the Presbyterian Church dates from 1755. Its pastors also included presidents of the college: Aaron Burr, Jonathan Edwards, and Samuel Davies. It was the college that gave the church the land

and the funds to build its first house of worship in 1762. Samuel Davies, the fourth president of the college, is credited with raising the funds in England and Scotland to build Nassau Hall. And during the Revolution the church was used as quarters by the British troops who turned the pews into firewood.

Above: Miller Chapel of Princeton Theological Seminary, designed by Charles Steadman in 1833. The chapel was originally located near the seminary's Alexander Hall and was moved to its present site in 1937. Dr. Samuel Miller was the seminary's second professor, after Dr. Archibald Alexander.

The interiors of the Nassau Presbyterian Church, formerly known as the First Presbyterian Church (*opposite, top*) and Miller Chapel (*opposite, bottom*). The Gothic apse of the University Chapel (*above*) soars majestically over neighboring structures. With the exception of two new towers, this is the tallest building on the campus.

St. Paul's Church (*opposite, top*), completed in 1957, replacing earlier structures built in 1850 and 1879 for the Roman Catholic community. Princeton's first Catholic chaplain came in 1798.

Princeton Baptist Church (*opposite, bottom*), built in 1812 and located in Penn's Neck, at the junction of Washington Road and Route One.

Trinity Church (*above*), built in 1868 and designed by R.M. Upjohn, son of the architect of New York's Trinity Church. This structure and the parish school building of 1849 evoke images of an old English country church. They replace an earlier Doric church built in 1833.

Above: The Kingston bridge was built in 1798 and until recently handled all traffic, including buses and trucks entering Princeton from the East. Washington destroyed the first stone bridge in 1777 on his retreat to Morristown after the Battle of Princeton in order to impede Cornwallis.

Opposite: The Kingston Presbyterian Church was organized in 1723, only twenty-five years after the congregation in Lawrence-ville was established, which is believed to be one of the oldest in the country. The present church building dates from 1852.

Kingston

Kingston is the town directly east of Princeton. It may have been settled earlier, and records show that Henry Greenland was a property owner in 1685, preceding Richard Stockton's purchase of Princeton land from William Penn by sixteen years. Between the two towns was the community of Queenston, located at the junction of Nassau and Harrison Streets. Today Kingston is joined to Princeton by a massive, stone arched bridge built in 1798.

Opposite, top: The settlement at Kingston on the Mill-stone River is one of the oldest between Trenton and New Brunswick.

Above: The first mill was built by Jacob Skillman in 1755 and was used continuously until it burned in 1888. The present building is on the original foundation.

Opposite, bottom: There were several mills located along the Millstone river that were demolished when Lake Carnegie was constructed—Aqueduct Mills (where the Delaware and Raritan Canal was carried over the Millstone on an aqueduct), Davison Mills, and Scudder's Mills.

Opposite, bottom: Sailing day on Lake Carnegie. Since the lake was opened in 1906, as a gift to Princeton University from Andrew Carnegie, it has been the scene of numerous aquatic sports, including rowing, canoeing, sailing, and windsurfing.

Opposite, top and above: Alongside the lake is the Delaware and Raritan Canal. Construction started in 1832 and the canal opened in 1834, financed largely by Robert Stockton and other Princetonians. All of the earth was removed by pick, shovel, and wheelbarrow. At its peak in 1859, it carried more tonnage than the Erie Canal with 1400 barges in operation between Trenton and New Brunswick. Large barges required up to twenty mules to tow them. Since there is only one towpath, it is interesting to imagine how the mules avoided becoming entangled in the lines of the oncoming barges. The answer lies in how the barges and mules passed each other. The barges passed port to port, or left side to left side, which is customary in traffic flows. The mules, however, passed on the right sides. One team would stop, and the momentum of its barges created enough slack for its lines to drop to the bottom of the canal. The other barge would glide over while its mules would step over the lines, passing on the inside of the other team.

Rowing began at Princeton in 1870, initially on the Delaware and Raritan Canal, as a deterrent to dissipation. In 1874, a boathouse was built and Princeton was admitted to the Rowing Association of American Colleges in spite of the objections of Amherst that "a line must be drawn somewhere." The crews were not very successful, because their training was on a narrow canal filled with barge traffic. Passing the barges was challenging, especially for the bow oar, who served as a coxswain and steered with his right foot as he rowed. Rowing skills improved dramatically with the opening of Lake Carnegie in 1906.

The Class of 1887 Boathouse (*right*) was built in 1913. The spectators are viewing a sprint from the Washington Road bridge. The adoption of the familiar orange and black as Princeton's colors is attributable to the crews of 1874. Until then all athletic teams wore something orange—a tradition started in 1868 in honor of King William III, House of Nassau and Prince of Orange. During the intercollegiate races at Saratoga, the freshman crew chalked black numerals on their orange shirts. A sportswriter added the tiger mascot some years later when Princeton football players wore socks and sleeves striped in orange and black.

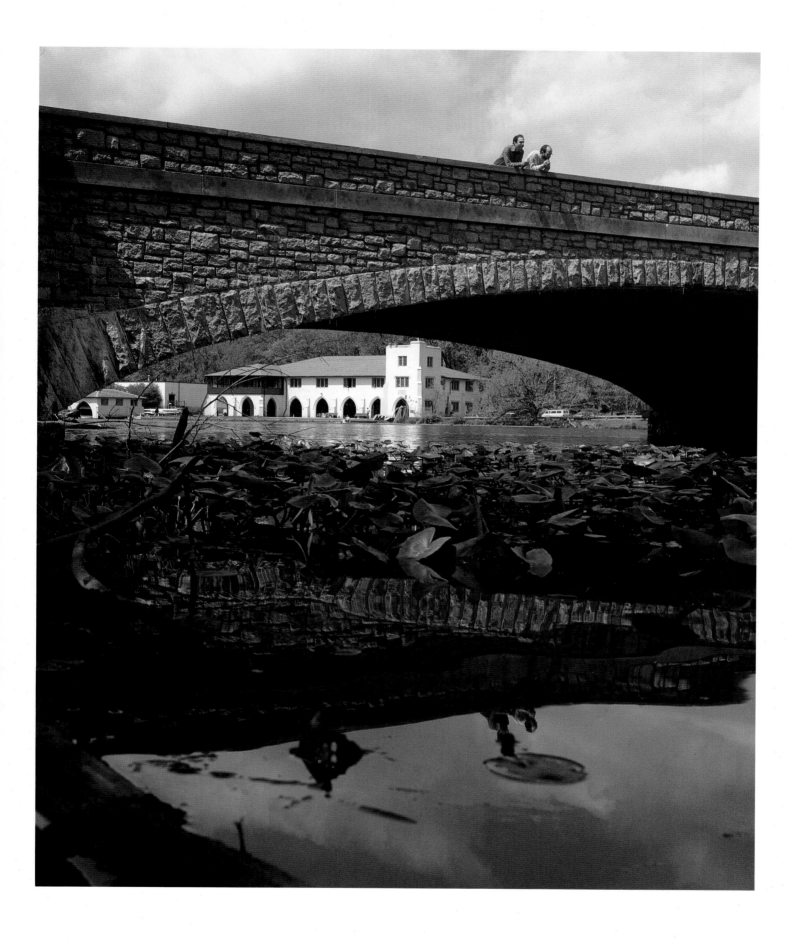

The Millstone River, after it has been transformed into Lake Carnegie.
Andrew Carnegie gave a lake that is three and a half miles long with a
two-thousand-yard straightaway rowing course that is considered one
of the finest in the East.

Cleveland Tower of the Princeton Graduate School designed by Ralph Adams Cram in 1913 and named in honor of Grover Cleveland, twenty-second and twenty-fourth President of the United States and university trustee from 1901 to 1908. The tower is reminiscent of Oxford's Magdalen Tower. At its dedication, President Taft praised its strength and beauty.

Schools and Research Centers

During the past several decades Princeton has become one the country's leading academic and research centers, in part because of its history, ambience, location, and university. The Institute for Advanced Study and the Westminster Choir College were drawn here in the early 1930s, and soon after that the Educational Testing Service, George Gallup's American Institute of Public Opinion, and the Robert Wood Johnson Foundation. By the 1950s RCA had established its David Sarnoff Research Center, AT&T its famous laboratories, and FMC and American Cyanamid had set up additional research facilities.

The broadening of the academic base began in 1810 when two institutions were created, each a leader in its field yet unrelated to the other and at opposite ends of the academic spectrum: the Princeton Theological Seminary and the Lawrenceville School. The seminary was proposed by the Presbytery of Philadelphia in 1810 as the first Presbyterian seminary in the United States. It began operations in 1812. The Lawrenceville School was proposed by Rev. Sir Isaac Brown, the Presbyterian minister in Maidenhead, as a school to provide high-quality education to sons of his congregation. Both institutions have grown to worldwide recognition for excellence in their respective fields in the past 175 years.

Among numerous research centers that have been established in Princeton are two unique institutions—the Institute for Advanced Study and the Center of Theological Inquiry. The Institute for Advanced Study is the first and largest residential institute of its kind in the country. It is designed for the pursuit of advanced research in the humanities and science. Of a more recent origin is the Center of Theological Inquiry which pursues common ties between theological and scientific studies, with the belief that all truth is essentially one, for all truth comes from God.

One of the most ambitious undertakings at present is the controlled development of the seventeen hundred acres on the Princeton Forrestal Center, adjacent to the university's Plasma Physics Laboratory. Discreetly tucked away in woodlands and landscaped grounds are some the country's largest corporate regional headquarters and research centers. The Johnson Foundation stands proudly at its entrance, while curving roads and careful spacing of the facilities give the visitor a sense of space and of the tasteful proportions of buildings, trees, and humans that prevails on the Princeton University campus itself. This is an excellent model of planned development of university property that has a sensitive eye to the future rather on maximizing the last dollar of today.

The Princeton University Graduate College

Thomson Court (*above*), the western entrance to the Princeton campus (*opposite, top*), and Wyman House, official residence of the dean of the graduate school (*opposite bottom*).

The graduate school, whose principal residence is the college, was established in 1900 but its antecedents reach back almost to Princeton's beginnings. James Madison, class of 1771, was the first graduate student. James McCosh laid the groundwork for a graduate school in 1868 and the school was officially established in 1900 with Andrew West, class of 1874, as its first dean. A difference evolved between university president Woodrow Wilson and Dean West over the location of the graduate college. West wanted it removed from the undergraduate campus and persuaded the widow of Senator John R. Thomson, class of 1817, and William Procter, class of 1883 and of Procter and Gam-

ble, to help locate the college on a site overlooking the golf course. Wilson felt that integration between undergraduate and graduate students would have been more beneficial, but by 1910 he withdrew from the university to campaign for, and win, the governorship of New Jersey and, in 1912, the presidency of the United States.

The graduate college was built in 1913 and expanded in 1927. Isaac Wyman, class of 1848, for whom the dean's residence is named, left his residuary estate for the development of the college. Over the fireplace in the dean's library hang the flintlock musket and powder horn that Wyman's grandfather used in the French and Indian Wars and which his father had carried in the Revolutionary Battle of Princeton at the age of sixteen.

Above: The Cleveland tower of the graduate school. This magnificent structure is 173 feet high and is easily spotted at some distance by travelers on Route One.

> *No Princeton man travelling that way ever fails, on pass-ing Princeton Junction, to glance with fondness towards what seems to him, more and more as his years roll on, a true oasis of rest and happiness in life's itinerary*
> —*Andrew F. West, Dean of the Graduate School*

Right: Faculty Housing on College Road, next to the Springdale Golf Course. This was a bequest of Ger-trude Winans Mathey, daughter of Samuel Ross Winans, Dean of the Faculty from 1899 to 1903. Funds were provided by Dean Mathey, class of 1912, a success-ful investment banker with Dillon, Read & Co. and trustee under presidents Hibben, Dodds and Goheen. The apartments were designed in 1952 by Dean Mathey's classmate, Arthur Holden, and resemble eighteenth-century quarters.

Above: "Springdale," 86 Mercer Street, the official residence of the president of Princeton Theological Seminary, and "Hodge House" (*left*). "Springdale" was built in the late 1840s by Richard Stockton, son of Commodore Robert Stockton. The name comes from the old Stockton farm on which the house and also the Springdale Golf Course are located. Unlike the Georgian symmetry of the earlier Stockton houses, "Springdale" is romantically picturesque, with an irregular silhouette and variety of ornament. "Hodge House," finished in 1825 for Charles Hodge of the seminary, is of more classical proportions. It includes a central Palladian window with a sunburst heading, which was a sophisticated element at the time for Princeton.

Princeton Theological Seminary

Alexander Hall, 1815 (*above*) and Brown Hall, 1865 (*right*). Alexander Hall is the first building erected by the Presbyterian Church in the United States for seminary purposes. It is considered to be one of the more charming and dignified structures in the East.

The theological seminary was founded in 1812 after the Presbyterian General Assembly voted in Philadelphia in 1810 that the college was becoming too secular in both its curriculum and general climate. For its part, the college felt the influence of the church was too restrictive. Upon separation from each other, the theo-logical seminary flourished with the support of the Presbyterian establishment. The college went into an eclipse from a lack of financial support, which only began to flow many years later because of the wealth and general concern of its alumni. The college eventually was able to regain its momentum. Today, the Princeton Theological Seminary is one of the leading seminaries in the world with approximately eight hundred students from many confessions and many countries. Its Speer Library is considered by many to be the best theological library in the world. The original mis-

sion of the seminary remains today: blending solid learning with piety of the heart, graduating scholars who are believers and believers who are scholars.

Reverend Dr. Archibald Alexander was the seminary's first professor. The building bearing his name was designed by John McComb, Jr., who also designed City Hall in New York and "Old Queens" at Rutgers University. It resembles Nassau Hall in many respects but is more proportioned. Both have a bold, simple, and dignified design that was suitable for their needs at the time and is still most relevant today.

Brown Hall, a student dormitory, was designed by J.P. Huber and was a gift of Mrs. George Brown in 1865. George Brown was a partner of the Baltimore investment banking firm of Alex. Brown & Sons. He and his father organized the Baltimore & Ohio Railroad Co. in 1827 and pioneered in the development of the passenger railway car. He and his wife, Isabella, were leaders in every important civic movement in Baltimore in their time.

Roberts Hall, named for Dr. Edward H. Roberts, dean of the seminary from 1945 to 1954. Roberts Hall was originally known as North and South Halls. The students at the seminary had at first boarded at Nassau Hall of the College of New Jersey. But Dr. Alexander soon had to report to his board of directors that "the number of students in college having so increased as to render the occupation of rooms by our students inconvenient, most of them, with their own consent, were removed to lodgings in the town, where they have been comfortably accommodated. It will be necessary, however, for the board to take some effectual measures to provide accommodations for the students in the future, as lodging rooms in the town are obtained with great difficulty."

The Aquinas Institute

The headquarters of this center of Catholic studies are at 65 Stockton Street in a house initially constructed for Archibald Russell but completed in 1907 for Henry Lane Eno of the Epsom Salts Company.

In the late 1930s Thomas Mann, winner of the 1929 Nobel Prize in Literature, accepted an appointment to lecture at the university and lived in this house. It was a short walk from the home of Albert Einstein, with whom he met frequently and with whom he had been friends in their native country. When Thomas Mann was made Doctor of Letters *honoris causa* in 1939 at a special ceremony, he expressed gratitude for his new home in America.

The Aquinas Institute was organized in 1928 as the Catholic Club by Dr. Hugh Taylor, dean of the Princeton Graduate School, and Mr. David McCabe, one of Woodrow Wilson's hand-picked preceptors. The name "Aquinas Institute" was adopted when the chaplaincy became a separate corporation with its own board of trustees. It is not a part of the university but does serve its students, faculty, and staff. Funding is provided by yearly appeals and weekly collections at the services; it is not supported by either the diocese or the university. The institute acquired its present headquarters building in 1953.

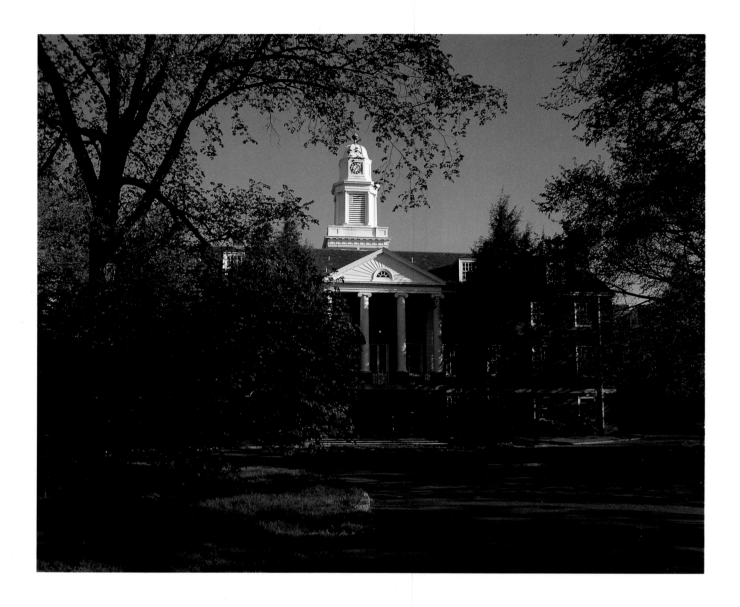

Westminster Choir College

This is the view of the college's Williamson Hall on Hamilton Avenue and Walnut Lane, named in honor of John Finley and Rhea Williamson who founded it in Ohio in 1925 and moved it to Princeton in 1932. It is a private nondenominational college of music located on a twenty-three acre campus, educating men and women at the undergraduate and graduate levels for careers in church music, teaching, and performance. Its four-year curricula lead to the Bachelor of Music degree. Present enrollment is approximately 400 from throughout the country, and alumni number 4,500. It is estimated that the college's alumni conduct over one million men, women, and children each week as church musicians and teachers in educational systems. The Westminster Choir has been performing since 1928 when it made the first coast-to-coast broadcast with the Cincinnati Symphony.

The Westminster Choir has performed with major orchestras and has sung over 300 performances with the New York Philharmonic. In 1929 it was the first American choir ever to appear in concert in England, in 1934 the first in the Soviet Union, and in 1957 it completed a tour of twenty-two countries under the U.S. Department of State's cultural exchange program. It sang on the Telstar World-Wide Telecast in the spring of 1964 for the opening of the New York World's Fair—reportedly the largest audience seeing a television show at the time—and in 1980 it was the first to be featured in the "Live from Lincoln Center" telecast series over national public television. Recently it participated in the ten-thousandth performance of the New York Philharmonic, the oldest permanent orchestra in the country.

The Center of Theological Inquiry.

This independent ecumenical research center, founded in 1978, is the first of its kind in the United States. Its main purpose is to find common bases of science and religion by bringing scholars from various academic disciplines together for a period of explanation and discussion. The center conducts research in the principal doctrines of theology and in the relationship among theology, science, and ethics. Its goal is to accomplish in theology what similar institutions are accomplishing in science and mathematics. Theological and scientific inquiry are pursued in the conviction that all truth is essentially one, for all truth comes from God. Faith is recognized by the center as the most basic form of knowledge from which all subsequent inquiry proceeds.

The main building at 50 Stockton Street was completed in 1984, designed by Michael Pardee Erdman and given by the Henry R. Luce Foundation. Mr. Luce was born in China to missionary parents; his father was an alumnus of Princeton Theological Seminary. Mr. Luce founded *Time*, *Life* and *Fortune* magazines and, throughout his life, was concerned about the lack of communication between science and religion. "While we have got science and religion fairly well distinguished from one another, we have not yet got them co-operating with one another. Where there should be only distinction, there is separation. The two affairs go on unrelatedly, whereas they should go on unitedly. The result is a certain impoverishment of both the religious and the scientific enterprise. The man of faith fails to know the full truth about this terrestrial universe, which is the concern of science. Conversely, the man of science fails to know the full truth about the destiny of man, which is the concern of religion."

Unless you believe, you will not understand.
Isaiah 7:9

St. Joseph's Preparatory Seminary

The seminary was founded in 1913 by the Congregation of the Mission of St. Vincent de Paul to educate young men for the priesthood of the Roman Catholic Church. It is one of the few residential high school seminaries in the country. Upon graduation, students enter Vincentian House and attend classes at St. John's University, both in New York.

The seminary traces its origins to St. Vincent de Paul, who established the Congregation of the Mission in 1625 to preach the gospel in France and train young men for the church. In 1816 they established a seminary in the Louisiana Territory, and in 1868 the central administrative office and graduate level program were moved to Philadelphia to become St. Vincent's Seminary. In order to provide adequate training for the graduate program, the Germantown Day College was founded in 1873; it became known as St. Vincent's Apostolic School in 1882 and moved to Princeton in 1913 as St. Joseph's College.

The seminary's campus includes several handsome buildings in the Gothic style, with face stones quarried on the property. The chapel (*above*) was built in 1934, designed by Ferdinand Durang of New York after the English Gothic style of the fourteenth century.

The Institute for Advanced Study

In 1930 Caroline and Louis Bamberger founded the Institute for Advanced Study for the pursuit of advanced learning and exploration in the fields of pure science and high scholarship. Today, the institute has Schools of Mathematics, Natural Sciences, Historical Studies, and Social Science.

The institute is independent of the university and yet maintains a symbiotic relationship with it. It awards no degrees and usually admits to membership scholars who have already received their highest degree. Members are admitted each year for short periods to pursue scholarly projects away from their normal duties at their home institutions. Approximately a third of its two hundred members come from Europe and Asia.

The institute is unique in several ways: it was the first such research institute in the United States and has been a model for many others which have since been established; it is the largest such residential institute in this country; and it combines both humanities and science—the cosmos of nature and the cosmos of culture. Albert Einstein, Erwin Panofsky and John von Neumann are among the institute's former faculty and visiting members. The institute's main building is Fuld Hall, built in 1939 by Jens Frederick Larson and named in honor of Caroline Bamberger Fuld.

The Mackenzie Administration Building as seen from the steps of the John Dixon Library. These twin buildings flanking Fathers' Building (at the left in the photograph) were inspired directly by Thomas Jefferson's "Monticello" and his University of Virginia. The administration building is named for James Cameron MacKenzie who was headmaster from 1883 to 1899. The John Dixon Library, which houses over 25,000 volumes, was named for a member of the board of trustees from 1890 to 1930. These handsome buildings were designed by William Delano, class of 1891.

Lawrenceville School

The school was founded in 1810 by Dr. Isaac Van Arsdale Brown, a Presbyterian minister who opened his front parlor to classes for nine local boys from his parish. Originally he called it the Academy of Maidenhead; the name was changed when the township was renamed Lawrenceville in 1816. Within four years of its founding it appeared that a new building was required, and in 1814, on a plot of land purchased for twenty-five dollars, the original section of the house now known as Hamill House was built. Students from as far away as the Carolinas and Georgia began to arrive, and by 1828 the student body included boarders from England, Cuba, and the Cherokee and Choctaw Nations.

By 1829 the school was known as the Classical and Commercial High School or simply Lawrenceville High School. The curriculum offered a "full and liberal course," emphasizing the classics and traditional methods of teaching by memorization and recitation. Dr. Brown also introduced a program, unusual at the time, of gymnastics and other exercises designed "to invigorate the physical system," and he offered a teacher for every ten boys, all living together as a family—a tradition that endures in principle today.

Alexander Hamilton Phillips, who came from one of Maidenhead's old families and was a cousin of the founders of the Exeter and Andover academies, became Dr. Brown's successor in 1834. Three years later Samuel Hamill became the headmaster of the school, a post he held for almost fifty years. Mr. Hamill was the first to establish the practice of avoiding a large number of written rules and regulations, relying instead on adherence to moral principles. This philosophy of avoiding hard and fast pronouncements and of not promulgating the final, absolute rule is practiced by the school today.

The next headmaster was Dr. James Cameron MacKenzie (1883–1899), who instituted the famous "house system," patterned after the English public schools. The trustees had sent him to England in 1882 to study the schools and educational systems. His report laid down the guidelines of the new campus, which called for several residences housing no more than twenty-four boys with a master and his family. A larger dormitory was to be built for the more mature boys, and these residences plus a classroom building and a new chapel were all to be strung around a central green. Under Dr. Mackenzie's leadership, and thanks to the estate of John Cleve Green, one of Dr. Brown's original nine students who endowed the school with $1,250,000 in 1879, the school grew in enrollment and physical facilities. Frederick Law Olmsted was retained to plan a new campus (he is best known for designing Central Park in New York) and Peabody and Stearns were retained to design the houses around "the Circle." The circle houses (Cleve, Dickinson, Griswold, Hamill, Kennedy, and Woodhall) provided small, homelike residences to members of the third and fourth forms (tenth and eleventh grades). The fifth form or senior class was united in a separate house called Upper House in an atmosphere that provided an independence similar to that of college life.

Dr. Mackenzie was succeeded by Dr. Simon John McPherson in 1899, who added a second form in 1904 and created the school's first student council. In his footsteps came one of Lawrenceville's best-known headmasters, Dr. Mather Abbot, who was known then and now as simply "the Bot." Dr. Abbot was headmaster from 1919 until 1934. Under his dynamic leadership the school built its lower school and library, Fathers' Building, and two new circle houses. Dr. Allan Heely succeeded to the office, continuing the vigorous momentum established by his predecessors. He adopted the conference plan of teaching utilizing the famous round tables, expanded the school's curriculum, and initiated an advanced placement program. New buildings were added under his leadership: the administration building, the field house, and the science buildings, among others.

In 1959 Dr. Bruce McClellan, who had been a teacher at the school for ten years, was chosen to succeed Dr. Heely. He led the school through the challenging period of social revolution in the late 1960s and early 1970s, resolutely championing responsible individuality, integrity of character, academic excellence, and the dignity of teaching. The latest chapter in the school's history is now just beginning. On January 3, 1985 the school's trustees voted to accept girls for the first time, in September 1987, and the school will also have a new head, Josiah Bunting, III.

Opposite: Hamill House (1814, 1827). This is one of six "circle houses" where students in the third and fourth form live with a housemaster. Lawrenceville's house system is unique among independent schools in this country and is patterned after English public schools like Rugby and Eton.

Hamill House is the school's oldest building, built four years after its founding. It is named for Samuel Hamill, who was the school's third headmaster, from 1837 until 1883. The stone came from the Cherry Grove quarry as did the stone for several of the pre-Revolutionary homes along the Lawrenceville Road or Main Street. With subsequent editions, Hamill houses forty-seven students and is the school's second largest house after Upper House.

Edith Memorial Chapel and afternoon games in "the Circle." The chapel was built in 1895, designed along with the eight other Victorian buildings around "the Circle," by Peabody and Stearns in the style of Henry Hobson Richardson. The plan of the chapel, which is named for the daughter of John C. Green—one of the school's most important benefactors—is that of a Latin cross, with a tower set at the front between the two arms. The transept windows are by Louis Tiffany and are filled with rich colors on sunny days.

Late afternoon is a popular time for a catch or game of frisbee in "the Circle." The school has one of the most extensive athletic facilities of any school its size in the country (ten baseball fields, nine footballs, nine soccer fields, its own golf course, twenty-three tennis courts, an enormous field house, hockey rinks and skeet shooting facilities).

The Allen P. Kirby Arts Center is the newest structure on "the Bowl," completed in 1962. It is named for a member of the class of 1913 who was a financier and trustee of the school from 1949 to 1967. The center has a fully equipped theater with a seating capacity of 890, as large as a Broadway theater, plus galleries and instructional rooms for the art department and the camera and art clubs.

Fathers' Building and "the Bowl." The six buildings around "the Bowl" were built between the late 1920s and mid-1930s. These Georgian-style buildings were designed by William Delano, class of 1891. Fathers' Building houses the departments of religion and foreign languages. It was a gift of the Fathers' Association in 1924.

The Hun School

The Hun School was founded in 1914 as the Princeton Math School, a tutorial school for Princeton University undergraduates, by John Gale Hun. In 1925 the name was changed to the Hun School and its curriculum was broadened to offer a general college preparatory program. Boarding facilities were provided to 150 boys on its Stockton Street campus. In that year it acquired "Edgerstoune," the former home of Archibald Russell and one of Princeton's grandest estates.

"Edgerstoune" (*opposite*) was completed in 1903 on an estate of 275 acres, part of William Penn's original holdings. The house is over two hundred feet long and ninety feet wide. There were ten master bedrooms and thirteen servants' rooms. Archibald Russell was a trustee of the university and a brother-in-law of Moses Taylor Pyne, whose "Drumthwacket" was the only other estate in town that could equal his in grandeur. Both Russell and Pyne traveled to New York and back on a private train, nor just a car, which they kept on a siding at the station, then below Blair Arch. Russell's wealth was largely inherited from his Scottish father. "Edgerstoune" was the last of the great Princeton mansions to be built and the first to pass out of residential use. The Hun School was its next owner.

In the years since 1925, the school has added six major buildings for classes, dining, boarding, athletics, and student activities. The lower school building was built in 1929 and now serves as part of the school's extensive athletic complex, one of the most comprehensive for any school its size. Girls were admitted as day students in 1971 and as boarders in 1975, comprising approximately a third of the student body today. A middle school was established in 1973. The school has an enrollment of approximately three hundred day and one-hundred sixty boarding students from fifteen states and twenty-five foreign countries. The foreign students enrich the cultural experiences of the student body, and each has a guardian residing in the United States who is able to assume responsibility for the student's affairs and take him or her into their homes during vacation periods. The day students provide a natural bridge for all boarders to home and community life, helping them establish contacts with townspeople and asking them home for visits with their families. The school's program and philosophy reflect the premise that intellectual growth occurs in the context of moral, social, and physical development, and that an education leading to college must embrace a range of activities and commitments beyond the classroom.

119

The Princeton High School

The High School's main facilities on Moore Street were built in 1928. The school traces its origins to the Princeton Model School, founded in 1857 and one of the first public schools in New Jersey. It became the Princeton High School in 1899 and was better known then as the Nassau Street School.

Presently there are over one thousand students enrolled in grades nine through twelve. The curriculum provides students with a variety of subjects from which to develop a program of studies commensurate with ability and interest. In addition to the basic course requirements, an extensive elective program is offered in the humanities, sciences, practical and creative arts. Some students study at the university and some university faculty give courses here. In recent years the High School has received top honors in national competitions in mathematics and science, has had approximately twenty percent of its senior class receiving

National Merit Scholarship semifinal or commended scholars recognition, and has sent approximately eighty percent of its students to four-year colleges, half of which are traditional Ivy League schools.

The High School also offers a wide variety of extra-curricular activities including approximately forty teams in eighteen different sports, assuring the student a variety of choice and competitive challenge, as well as four student publications and seventeen other clubs or activities. Students are encouraged to view learning as taking place both within and outside the classroom, and therefore extra-curricular activites are considered an integral part of the program. *Live to Learn and Learn to Live* is the school's motto which may be found over its main entrance door.

121

Princeton Day School

The school was founded in 1965 as a result of the merger of Miss Fine's School for girls (founded in 1894) and Princeton Country Day School for boys (founded in 1924). It is an independent day school enrolling approximately 850 boys and girls from junior kindergarten through the twelfth grade.

Princeton Day School has several handsome Georgian buildings on its Great Road estate, including "Colross," a manor house built by Jonathan Swift in 1799 in Alexandria, Virginia (*above*). Swift did not own the land on which the house was built, and it passed to the Alexander family upon his death in order to settle his indebtedness. Gustavus Alexander lost the house in a gambling debt to Thomas Mason, who in turn fell into hard times. The house was in a state of disrepair when Mrs. John R. Munn purchased it in 1929 and moved it, brick by brick, to Princeton. It was re-erected on a tract of land adjacent to one given to Princeton Day

School by Mr. and Mrs. Dean Mathey in 1963. The school acquired "Colross" shortly thereafter and uses it for some school offices and classrooms.

The school's mission is to offer students of above-average potential an exceptional opportunity for intellectual development, self-realization, and moral growth. It seeks to instill in its students an excitement about learning, a confidence in their own creativity, a concern for others, and sense of commitment. The school draws on the resources of Princeton University, the research organizations in the community, and the variety of Princeton residents to supplement its academic program.

Upon graduation students enroll at a wide variety of colleges and universities, with approximately a quarter of the class being either semifinalists or commended scholars in the National Merit Scholarship Program.

Chapin School

This school, founded in 1931 by Frances Chapin, is located on the Princeton Pike near Lawrenceville. The central classroom building was built around 1740 by a member of the Theophilus Phillips family, one of the original settlers of Lawrence township. Chapin presently has four buildings on seven acres of the original Phillips property. The school enrolls approximately 225 boys and girls from kindergarten through the eighth grade from local communities in the Central New Jersey–Bucks County, Pennsylvania area. Upon graduation they attend, for the most part, independent schools in the area: Hun, Lawrenceville, Peddie, Pennington, and Princeton Day School.

The school's mission is to maintain a supportive environment enabling the students to develop a sense of belonging, enthusiasm, and self-confidence. The philosophy of the school is predicated on the belief that a child's attitude toward learning directly affects his or her performance. Chapin is committed to the development of the whole child—not just intellectual but social, emotional, physical, and moral as well.

Chapin prefers a mix of academic, social, and economic backgrounds, believing that children learn from each other as well as from their teachers. The school tries to offer the broadest possible experience for its students and its graduates range from research scientists to taxi drivers, from Broadway actors to sea captains, from divinity students to professional soccer players.

Stuart Country Day School
of the Sacred Heart

This is one of the community's youngest schools, founded in 1963 as a member of the Network of Sacred Heart Schools (there are nineteen throughout the country). Stuart Country Day is one of the few secondary schools in the country devoted exclusively to the education of women. It has approximately 420 students from pre-kindergarten through twelfth grade. Boys are enrolled only at the pre-school level.

Although grounded in the Roman Catholic tradition, Stuart Country Day is not a parochial school. It is a private, independent school with slightly less than 50 percent of its student body Roman Catholic. The education is competitive with the finest in the country but with an emphasis on educating the person with deep Christian values. Girls go on to a wide range of colleges, which last year included Cornell, Dartmouth, Harvard, and Wellesley (as well as Princeton).

The main building of Stuart Country Day was designed by Jean Labatut and incorporates many religious symbols such as water and light as well as a stark representation of the Sacred Heart. The boulders are probably glacial remains on the property and have been incorporated in the building both inside and out. Large glass windows also bring the woodlands indoors, and the result is a building of warmth and openness that is cheerful for the children to study in.

Opinion Research Corporation

This corporation was established in 1938 by Dr. Claude Robinson, an associate director of the Gallup Poll. It is the largest survey-based organization in Princeton and has pioneered in the founding and evolution of public opinion research. Its primary mission is to provide survey research and management consulting services to business, industry, government, and academia. Opinion Research Corporation employs two hundred full-time and three hundred part-time professionals in the broad range of market research, public issues, social science, government, and organizational behavior. In 1985 it conducted approximately five hundred research projects.

Educational Testing Service

Educational Testing Service (ETS) is a private, non-profit corporation devoted· to measurement and research, primarily in education. It was founded in 1947 by the American Council on Education, the Carnegie Foundation for the Advancement of Teaching, and the College Entrance Examination Board.

The College Board, a membership organization of approximately 2,500 colleges and schools, hires ETS to develop and administer its Scholastic Aptitude Test (SAT), taken by about 1.5 million college-bound high school juniors and seniors each year. The firm also develops and administers the Advanced Placement Examinations and scores them during a six-day period each spring when 1,200 teachers read approximately 300,000 essays, the Preliminary Scholastic Aptitude Test (the qualifying test for the National Merit Scholarships), Secondary School Admission Test, the Graduate Record Examinations, the Graduate Management Admission Test, licensing examinations for the real estate and insurance industries, and other tests measuring knowledge, skills, and aptitudes.

The headquarters building was built in 1958, designed by Harrison, Abramowitz & Abbe, and named for James Bryant Conant, first chairman of the ETS board of trustees, former president of Harvard University, and former U.S. ambassador to the Federal Republic of Germany.

AT&T's Engineering Research Center

The headquarters of American Telephone & Telegraph Company's Engineering Research Center on Carter Road are located in an early nineteenth century manor house (*opposite*) and a Skidmore, Owings & Merrill facility built in 1962 (*above*). The Engineering Research Center first opened in 1958 and is the first research laboratory in the world devoted solely to manufacturing technology. Part of the center's work is to find more efficient and less expensive methods of making the company's products. The center's researchers have received over five hundred and fifty patents in such areas as advanced automation, light energy, semiconductor processes, testing, engineering computer aids and interconnection technologies. The center has been the first to develop industrial uses of lasers and has pioneered in lightware technology, silicon growing and robotics. The staff of the Engineering Research Center is composed of members with diverse scientific and engineering backgrounds.

The parent of the center is American Telephone and Telegraph Company, organized in 1885 as the successor to the American Bell Telephone Company. Messrs. Alexander Bell and Thomas Watson had successfully tested the telephone in 1875. The telephone and AT&T developed rapidly and resulted in the largest company in the world, as measured by assets, at

128

the time of the reorganization in 1984. The following chronology of selected events shows the rapid growth of this communications company: 1879—the first use of telephone numbers for the more than 200 subscribers in Lowell, Massachusetts; 1881—the first commercially successful long distance line (between Boston and Providence); 1896—the first use of telephones with rotary dials; 1915—transcontinental service operated between Philadelphia and San Francisco with the ringing of the Liberty Bell; 1922—the first football game broadcast (Princeton's defeat of the University of Chicago, 21-18) was carried by wire hook-up to New York; 1929—transatlantic service opened to Berlin, Paris, Madrid and Prague; 1935—the first round-the-world call was made; 1948—the first public demonstration of the transistor by Bell Telephone Laboratories was held; 1951—direct long distance dialing began; 1962—the first "skyphone" service began on TWA; 1965—commercial telephone service with Europe via satellite began. From its modest beginning, AT&T had almost 900,000 telephones in service by 1900, 50 million by 1952 and 90 million by 1969. At present there are many more than that in service. Just prior to the 1984 reorganization, American Telephone & Telegraph Company had sales of $64.1 billion and assets of $149.5 billion—the largest company in the world.

David Sarnoff Research Center

This famous laboratory was built by RCA Corporation on a 350-acre site on Route One in 1942. It was designed by Harrry L. Porter and named for the company's founder.

Among the noteworthy products that have been developed here are the shadow-mask color television picture tube in 1949 which made possible the production of hundreds of millions of color television receivers. The development of the all-electronic, compatible color television system has set the standard in the western hemisphere. RCA Laboratories in Princeton has pioneered other major advances in electronics in the past forty years including high-fidelity stereo, high-speed memories for computers, injection lasers, liquid-crystal displays, high-capacity satellite communications, MOS transistors, logic arrays, and both optical and capacitive video disc systems.

RCA Corporation was organized in 1919 at the request of the U.S. Navy to develop a domestically-owned international communications company. General Electric Company, which was RCA's first major shareholder, has acquired RCA in a recent merger and is transferring the research center to SRI International.

SRI International was founded in 1946 by Stanford University as the Stanford Research Institute. In 1977 it became an independent, non-profit corporation and changed its name to SRI International. SRI is a research, development and consulting organization with offices and laboratories throughout the world. It employs nearly 3000 professionals working in more than 100 areas of knowledge. SRI is responsible for such innovations as the magnetic ink character recognition system which revolutionized check handling for banks, the remote cursor control used on many personal computers, and various medical diagnostic devices.

FMC Corporation

The FMC Corporation Research and Development Center, designed by H.K. Ferguson, was opened in 1956. FMC Corporation, whose name comes from Food Machinery and Chemical Corporation, was one of the first companies to come to the Princeton area, attracted by its ambience, its proximity to New York and Philadelphia, and by the university and other research institutions.

The company's origins go back to 1884 when a California engineer, John Bean, invented the first effective pressure pump for spraying orchards. Today the company is still manufacturing spraying, dusting and fogging equipment. It also manufactures harvesting and processing equipment with which food can be picked and prepared for canning or freezing on the combine. It makes earth moving equipment, and it makes selected defense items for the U.S. Government. With 1985 sales of $3.3 billion, FMC Corporation employs 27,000 people worldwide and is the thirtieth largest exporter in the United States.

There are approximately 725 employees at the Princeton Research Center, concentrating on research for the manufacturing, chemical, and agricultural industries. Many well-known insecticides and herbicides have been developed here as well as major basic "building blocks" for the chemical industry.

131

The James Forrestal Research Campus

The Plasma Physics Laboratory (*above*), located on Princeton University's 500-acre James Forrestal Research Campus, is designed to test the feasibility of using nuclear fusion to produce energy. It is a result of Project Matterhorn, which the university undertook in the 1950s with the U.S. Atomic Energy Commission to create nuclear in plasma (*ionized gases*) similar to what was occurring naturally in the sun. The process is based on Einstein's famous equation, $E = MC^2$. Mass can be converted into energy, and by two methods: *fission*, where the nuclei of heavy atoms are split apart and the energy that holds them together is released, and *fusion* (the sun's way) where the nuclei of light atoms are joined together, giving off even more energy

as they do so. At this Princeton facility the plasma is contained in a magnetic field (regular materials would melt) and heated to 100 million degrees centigrade, six times greater than the core of the sun.

Sayre Hall (*above*), built in 1932 as one of the original James Forrestal Research Campus facilities and named for the first director of the campus. James Forrestal, class of 1915, was the country's first secretary of defense from 1947 to 1949. In addition to research in aerospace and mechanical science, the campus also conducts theoretical research in meteorology and oceanography.

133

Princeton Forrestal Center

This is a 1750-acre residential, research, and corporate office park owned by the university. It is one of the largest and oldest university-related research parks in the country. Its aim is to attract a variety of companies that will enhance the community in many different ways. Since the 1970s, major tenants have included Dow Jones & Company, IBM Corporation, Merrill Lynch & Company, Prudential Insurance Company, RCA Corporation, and the Robert Wood Johnson Foundation. Presently under construction is a new super computer estimated to cost approximately $100 million and financed largely by a grant from the National Science Foundation. Partners with Princeton University in the project are twelve other universities including Brown, Columbia, Harvard, the Institute for Advanced Study, M.I.T., New York University, Penn, and Rutgers. It will be one of five super computer centers in the country.

Forrestal Center has been a successful undertaking for the university, which has concentrated on real-estate rather than academic connections with these corporations. It has made an unusual commitment to preserve approximately a third of its acreage as permanent open space. Foliage and fields add a peaceful tone to this research park.

The Robert Wood Johnson Foundation

Located at the entrance to the Princeton Forrestal Center is the headquarters building of the Robert Wood Johnson Foundation, designed by Brown & Matthews and completed in 1976. The Foundation was established in 1936 by General Robert Wood Johnson, son of one of the founders of Johnson & Johnson and its chief executive officer from 1932 until 1963.

Johnson & Johnson was founded in 1886 in New Brunswick to manufacture antiseptic surgical dressings. It is best known for the Band-Aid, introduced in 1921, and a line of baby care products which were introduced earlier. Today Johnson & Johnson consists of 165 affiliates and subsidiaries, and with 1985 sales of $6.4 billion is the most diversified health care company in the world. Its headquarters are several miles north of the Johnson Foundation on Route One.

The Robert Wood Johnson Foundation is an independent, not-for-profit corporation governed by its own board of trustees. Its endowment is approximately the size of Princeton University's—$1.8 billion. The Foundation is the largest private foundation operating solely in the field of health, and it is one of the ten largest foundations in the world in total assets. Last year grants totalling $65.9 million were made to groups working to improve health care in the United States. Independent surveys judge the Robert Wood Johnson Foundation to be a model for large foundations in terms of integrity, management, social sensitivities, clarity and ambitiousness of its purpose, and overall intellectual judgement governing its strategy and grant making decisions.

135

Prudential Insurance Company—
Enerplex North and Enerplex South

This dual, energy-saving structure of 269,000 square feet, called Enerplex North and Enerplex South, was built by the Prudential Insurance Company in 1983, one of many properties it has built in the area. Enerplex North (*above*) was designed by Skidmore, Owings & Merrill and Enerplex South by the university's School of Architecture and Urban Planning.

Enerplex North has an enclosed atrium across the entire south facade, as shown in the photograph. Sun shades allow the winter sun to pass through but block the summer sun. Warmed air from the winter sun is retained and redistributed throughout the building. On the east, north and west sides are double layer glass

walls. The glass panels are eighteen inches apart creating an insulating air jacket. Enerplex North also uses an ice pond for cooling purposes in the summer. This is a reincarnation of the familiar New England ice house. In the winter, the pond's domed cover is opened and a snow-making machine creates slush ice. In the summer, the dome is closed. Cold water is drawn from the bottom of the pond and circulated through a heat exchange coil, eliminating the need for air conditioning.

Enerplex North is occupied by RCA Corporation and Enerplex South by Dow Jones & Company and others.

136

Scanticon-Princeton Executive Conference Center and Hotel

Located on a twenty-five-acre wooded site in the For-restal Center, this 400-bed facility has thirty-seven meeting rooms. The hotel is operated by Scanticon International, Inc., based in Princeton. It was designed by Friis & Moltke and opened in 1981. The first Scanti-con (which means Scandinavian Conference Center) opened in Denmark's second largest city, Aarhus, in 1969.

Scanticon-Princeton has received top ratings in vari-ous travel guidebooks and was voted one of the eight best conference centers in the country by a national meetings trade publication. It has three restaurants, extensive athletic facilities and state-of-the-art audio-visual equipment. Several additional Scanticon Confer-ence Centers are planned around the country.

IBM Corporation

This is one of several facilities leased by IBM Corpora-tion at the Forrestal Center. It was modified for IBM by Hanes, Lundberg & Waehler in 1981. IBM employs approximately fifteen hundred in the Princeton area, engaged primarily in marketing and direct response operations, as well as distribution of IBM products and servicing of personal computers.

The Computing-Tabulating-Recording Company adopted the name International Business Machines Corporation in 1924. Thomas J. Watson, Sr. had joined C-T-R in 1914. Today IBM Corporation devel-ops, manufactures, markets and services information processing systems on a worldwide basis. Recent sales were approximately $50.1 billion and total employees were 405,535.

Merrill Lynch & Co., Inc.

Bordering on the Bee Pond at the southern edge of the Princeton Forrestal Center is the Merrill Lynch Corporate Campus. This is a conference and training center, with overnight accommodations. It also houses adminstrative and asset management departments for Merrill Lynch. The center opened in 1986 and was designed by the Kling Partnership. Approximately sixteen hundred people are employed here.

The Merrill Lynch & Co. name was adopted on October 15, 1915 as a successor to the firm started by Charles E. Merrill in 1914. Edmund Lynch joined later that year. Messrs. Merrill and Lynch felt there were many potential investors outside the social and economic elite catered to by the old-line Wall Street houses. They also pioneered in raising capital for the emerging chain store industry such as Kresge's and McCrory's. In fact the McCrory offering had to be sold twice because the outbreak of war in Europe in 1914 caused the New York Stock Exchange to close for four

months during the middle of the firm's offering. It was subsequently reoffered the following year.

The firm hired Wall Street's first bond saleswoman in 1919, Annie Grimes, opened its uptown New York office every weekday evening from 7 P.M. to 9 P.M. beginning in 1924, in order to cater to the "average investor," and continued to concentrate on raising capital for the retail chains. In 1930, Merrill, Lynch transferred most of its business to E.A. Pierce & Co., founded in 1885 and by then the nation's largest wire house. During the 1920s, Pierce had established branches across the country, connected by a network of private wires to transmit orders and quotations. In 1940 Charles Merrill was persuaded to combine Merrill Lynch with Pierce to create a new style of brokerage company intent on "bringing Wall Street to Main Street."

In 1941 Merrill Lynch was the first Wall Street firm to issue an annual report showing its operating results

for the year. Also in that year it merged with Fenner & Beane which resulted in offices in 92 cities around the country. In 1955 the firm was selected as one of seven managers of the initial public offering for Ford Motor Company, giving Merrill Lynch its first billion-dollar underwriting year. Also in 1955 the firm became one of the first American businesses to computerize its operations with the purchase of three IBM 650s, and it was the first Wall Street firm to install the more powerful, second generation, transistorized IBM 7080. During the late 1960s the surge in trading volume on the New York Stock Exchange caught many firms unprepared for the commensurate paperwork. Trade confirmations and securities certificates were lost, and by the second half of 1970, numerous major firms were on the verge of collapse or had already gone under. In October, 1970, the fifth largest member firm was about to fail. Had it done so the Exchange would have had a serious panic and therefore Merrill Lynch was asked to step in to absorb the floundering Good-body & Co. Merrill Lynch was the only firm capable of handling such an acquisition. By 1971 it had digested the assignment and was ready to sell its shares to the public for the first time. It was the second Exchange member to do so after Donaldson, Lufkin & Jenrette. In April, 1978 the firm acquired the prestigious, old-line investment banking house of White, Weld & Co.

Today Merrill Lynch has approximately 12,500 registered representatives in over 500 offices throughout the world. Its equity capital is approximately $2.5 billion making it the largest and clearly one of the most successful investment banking and securities firms in the country, based on the primary objective of serving the investment and financial needs of individuals and institutions.

Dow Jones & Company, Inc.

This is the regional headquarters for the famous publishing firm organized in 1881 by Charles Henry Dow and Edward Jones. Their first financial newsletter was called the *Customers' Afternoon Letter* which evolved into *The Wall Street Journal* by 1889. By 1884 they had started another important element of American financial information—the Dow Jones Average, consisting of eleven stocks listed on the New York Stock Exchange. *Barron's National Business and Financial Weekly* was started in 1921 with Clarence Barron as its first editor. The tabloid was an immediate success and reached a circulation of 30,000 in its sixth year.

The architect of the today's *Journal* was Barney Kilgore who became managing editor in 1941. He turned the financial newspaper into one that encompassed all aspects of business, economics and consumer affairs as well as everything else that had an impact on business.

Research facilities established in South Brunswick in the early 1960s led to a series of production breakthroughs including microwave transmission of full page images from plant to plant. Today these images are beamed via satellite from the Dow Jones composing plant in Chicopee, Massachusetts and other plants, to regional centers such as Princeton. With a paid circulation of approximately 2.1 million, *The Wall Street Journal* is the largest newspaper in the United States.

The Princeton facility was built in 1965 and designed by John Graham. At this location are approximately eight hundred employees involved in the preparation and printing of both *The Wall Street Journal* and *Barron's* as well as the administration of information services, News/Retrieval, operating services, plant communications and production facilities, and accounting, auditing and payroll services for all of Dow Jones.

Squibb Corporation

This is the world headquarters of the pharmaceutical company founded in 1858 by Dr. Edward Robinson Squibb in Brooklyn. Dr. Squibb was a former navy surgeon who developed a process for the manufacture of pure, consistently high-grade ether and other medicines. Impure drugs were a problem at the time, and at the request of the government, Dr. Squibb established and served as a director of a laboratory of the Naval Hospital of Brooklyn before forming his own company. Dr. Squibb also proposed the standards included in the Pure Food and Drug Act which was passed in 1906, six years after his death.

Squibb anesthetics were widely used during World War I, and in 1938 the Squibb Institute for Medical Research was founded in New Brunswick, one of the first centers of its kind in the world. From the first crys-

tallization of penicillin and development of giant-tank fermentation to the creation of an entirely new class of synthetic monobactams, Squibb scientists have excelled in antibiotic research. Today the company offers approximately 1,000 pharmaceuticals derived from this research including cardiovascular agents, antibiotics, hormones and insulins, as well as health care products and medical equipment.

The company employs approximately 24,000 people worldwide including approximately 1,000 at its headquarters. This building, on the Princeton-Lawrenceville Road, was designed by Gyo Obata and opened in 1971. It is located on 273 acres, fronting on a twelve-acre lake, and it contains one of the most beautiful corporate art galleries in the country.

Princeton University

Princeton, like its predecessors Harvard, William & Mary and Yale, was established by the church. And for the past two hundred years its presidents have either been Presbyterians or sons of ministers. Princeton has several distinctive features that place it among the finest liberal arts universities in the world. First, its large endowment enables it to keep one of the lowest student to faculty ratios in the world (about 1:4). Second, it is committed to the education of both undergraduate and graduate students by a single faculty. Third, under Woodrow Wilson the university introduced both the preceptorial system, where students and faculty were brought together in small discussion groups as a routine part of the educational system, as well as the honor system, which places the responsibility of honorable behavior in exams and elsewhere on the students themselves. Fourth, Wilson also continued the example, established by his predecessors, of training undergraduates to serve, whether in the political arena or in the private sector. And fifth is the environment in which the university is located—small, beautiful, and surrounded by reminders of an important historical past.

Princeton is a residential university, unlike the majority of universities around the world, where students live at home and travel back and forth to classes. Even in the United States less than half of those attending four-year universities live on a campus. Residential life at Princeton is not an appendage to the academic program, President William Bowen reminds incoming students, but a conscious program to develop all a student's capacities—including the capacities to learn, to live a full life, and to serve others. It is based on the assumption that transactions in the classroom, important as they are, should be supplemented with the experience of living with others of different backgrounds. "We believe that education should open minds rather than try to fill them up," Bowen says, "that it should prepare students to appreciate the beauty of ideas as well as the world around them, to understand both other people and themselves, and to be effective citizens in a democracy. We aim to educate the whole person."

The American system of private education is unique in the world, achieving a very broad range of goals in educating the individual, through a combination of

The northern edge of the university campus and Nassau Street. Holder Tower, now part of Rockefeller College, was built in 1910. Like its larger companion, Cleveland Tower at the Graduate College, this tower is a visible and well-recognized landmark. Immediately to the right of Holder Tower is Madison Hall, the dining commons for Rockefeller College, also built in 1910 and named for President James Madison, class of 1771, father of the Constitution and the Bill of Rights. Madison was also, in later years, the first president of the Princeton Alumni Association.

Just to the right of the university buildings are town offices including those of the *Town Topics*, one of the community's newspapers.

public and private resources. Princeton has been able to maintain its academic freedom, which is any university's most treasured possession, because of its large endowment from loyal alumni. At $1.9 billion, Princeton's capital is third in the country behind Harvard's $2.3 billion and the University of Texas' $2 billion, but with a combined undergraduate and graduate student population of 6,000, compared with 15,600 for Harvard and 48,000 for Texas, Princeton has the largest endowment per capita of these major universities. Unlike state universities, Princeton is not beholden to the general public and their various demands. It has had greater freedom in deciding what kind of institution it wishes to be and has chosen to offer a liberal and scientific education of highest quality to a very select group of students. Its facilities verge on the luxurious and although its tuition is high, there is liberal financial aid to supplement the heavily endowed program.

The faculty includes scholars of national reputations and is at the complete disposal of the undergraduates. Professional schools are not as numerous as at the large state universities, for Princeton has chosen to concentrate on such areas as mathematics, art and archeology, international affairs, nuclear physics, and engineering. Yet in spite of its achievements in the growing graduate programs, Princeton continues to focus more than any other Ivy League university on the undergraduates: they still come first. The four thousand undergraduates are Princeton's primary concern, and there is perhaps no other university in the country where such a distinguished faculty gives so much of its time to them. The desired product is still the same today as it was in the days of John Witherspoon— a liberal education of the individual, the personal quest for knowledge and self-mastery, and the desire to play an integral part in the community.

For over two hundred years Princeton alumni have consistently assumed leading roles in shaping American history. John Witherspoon came from Scotland to be its president in 1768, twenty-two years after it was founded as the College of New Jersey in 1746. He was a staunch advocate of the rights of independent thinking, was the only minister to sign the Declaration of Independence, and during his tenure produced thirty-nine representatives, twenty-one senators, twelve governors, a vice president and a president (Madison). During the Revolutionary War, Witherspoon moved the college out of Nassau Hall, which then became a barracks for both British and U.S. troops (in succession). After the war the Congress fled to Princeton in 1783 because of a fear of mutiny by the troops over back wages which the Treasury was unable to pay. During the summer the Congress met continuously to work out peace arrangements and to tackle other programs in foreign and Indian affairs. For the commencement exercises that year, held as customarily in the fall, attending on September 24, 1783 were not only President Witherspoon, the trustees, and the graduating class but also the entire U.S. Congress and George Washington. Congress adjourned on November 1, and left Princeton shortly after-

Holder courtyard, located on the original four and a half acres of land donated to the college by Nathaniel FitzRandolph. He was the primary organizer of the citizens of Princeton in raising the money and land that the college's trustees required for a new location—£1,000 New Jersey money, ten acres of cleared land for the campus, and two hundred acres of woodland for fuel. Through FitzRandolph's efforts, Princeton was chosen over New Brunswick in 1753 as the new site for the college. Twelve years later New Brunswick became the home of the eighth college organized in this country before the Revolution: Queens College, also known as Rutgers.

A Gothic arch frames the original FitzRandolph
grounds of Rockefeller College.

wards. Nassau Hall ceased to be the nation's capital.

The after-war period was one of a rise and fall in enrollment, finances, and morale. The Presbyterian General Assembly, saddened at the decline in the number of alumni entering their ministry, voted in 1810 to establish a separate theological seminary. With this move the college's finances went into disarray—cut off from English support after the war and now from the church. The college was forced to turn more quickly to its alumni for support than most other colleges. By 1826 the Alumni Association of Nassau Hall was founded by James Maclean with James Madison as its first president. These alumni associations were an American idea. Princeton was not the first to be organized but did set the example in later years to which other universities aspired.

During the early nineteenth century the college experienced a period of controlled anarchy, with students resisting all rules, regulations, and the evangelical preaching of the faculty. Athletics were only organized later as an outlet for the students' energies; in fact one of the first gymnasiums in the country was built here in 1859. In 1868 the college once again turned to Scotland for presidential leadership as it had a hundred years earlier. James McCosh took control, and in twenty years doubled the endowment, tripled the college's acreage and facilities, and increased faculty salaries. Most important, McCosh increased the image of the college, which continued under Woodrow Wilson. The financial success of its alumni and the enhanced reputation of the college resulted in an increase in the momentum of contributions. This was the development that propelled Princeton from behind to one of the leading universities—now on a par with Harvard and Yale. The name was changed from the College of New Jersey to Princeton University at its sesquincentennial in 1896.

The change to a university came when other major colleges were also changing. The impetus was coming from several directions: from the establishment of major land-grant colleges in the Midwest and elsewhere, the influence of the German universities with broader curricula requiring professors to specialize and not try to be universally capable in everything, and the Darwinian theory of evolution, which elevated the position of science. These trends broadened the scope of the educational program at Princeton, which decided to expand as well as add graduate studies. Woodrow Wilson moved Princeton into the public limelight. He was the first non-minister president and called his inaugural address "Princeton in the Nation's Service"—not the church's service. He introduced the preceptorial system with the selection of fifty preceptors to meet with students in small groups. This is considered to be his greatest contribution to higher education in this country. Woodrow Wilson also revamped the program of study, with the first two years being well structured and the last two being open for concentration in a major of one's choice. His greatest defeat came in his inability to establish residential colleges and a graduate school on, rather than separate from, the main campus. The former is being implemented now and the latter has become well-intertwined with the rest of the university. Wilson went on to greater achievements.

Alumni contributions continued to pour in, and under President Hibben, from 1912 to 1932, the university entered a building program unparalleled anywhere else at the time, firmly establishing the Gothic style as the accepted one for American universities. The mood on the campus during these years was generally relaxed but it changed in the 1950s and 1960s as students became concerned about career objectives and training for graduate schools. Women were first admitted in 1969, another milestone event. But with continued growth and change there remain two important themes: the desire for excellence and the preservation of tradition. The expectation of doing well is taken for granted at Princeton, and those who excel are not particularly noticed. The individual is constantly proving him- or herself even after admission. But the anchor to windward is Princeton's firm hold on tradition. Change here is evolutionary. There is a continuous review of the past to keep the best of the old in order to sail most effectively into the future. It is what helps to keep Princeton from becoming anything less than Princeton.

Nassau Hall, built between 1754 and 1756 (*opposite*). At the time of its completion it was the largest stone building in America. At the suggestion of the governor of the province of New Jersey it was named in memory of King William III of England, House of Nassau and also Prince of Orange.

Nassau Hall was designed by Robert Smith of Philadelphia. Its walls are twenty-six inches thick and have enabled it to withstand two years of military occupation during the Revolution (by both American and British troops, who burned the college's entire library for fuel), plus the devastating fires of 1802 and 1855 and the antics of students (who were fond of setting off explosives and running occasional horse races in the upper corridors). After the Revolution, Nassau Hall served as a refuge for the Continental Congress from July to October of 1783, and it was here that they received news of the signing of the definitive peace treaty with Great Britain. The first foreign minister accredited to the United States was received here. He came from the Netherlands.

During the 1783 congressional session, the trustees of the college asked George Washington to sit for a portrait by Charles Willson Peale, which they placed in the prayer hall in a frame that had been occupied by a portrait of King George II. It is one of the few life portraits of Washington.

In 1802, a fire gutted the interior of Nassau Hall and the trustees turned to Benjamin Henry Latrobe, the first professional architect in the United States (Robert Smith was an architect/carpenter). Raising funds for its repair proceeded right away, with the town of Princeton making the first contribution, in part out of fear that the college might move elsewhere after its only major building was destroyed. Latrobe concentrated on fireproof improvements—brick floors rather than wooden ones, stone stairs with iron railings, and, for the first time in this country, an experimental sheet-iron roof. Further fire-prevention modifications were made by John Notman after another serious fire in 1855. At this time the prayer room on the south side was expanded.

149

Blair Hall, 1897 (*right*) and the Princeton Junction and Back train (*above*). Blair Hall was designed by Cope and Stewardson of Philadelphia and is considered to be their finest example of Tudor Gothic. This building, together with Little Hall, built in 1899, established the trend towards Gothic architecture on the American college campus.

John Insley Blair, a trustee of the college from 1866 to 1899, gave the funds for Blair Hall. He was a co-founder of the Delaware, Lackawanna and Western Railroad and later the Union Pacific Railroad. At one time he owned more miles of railroad rights-of-way than any other person. Of modest education, he said,

when asked about his generous philanthropy to Princeton, that he had spent most of his life learning addition, but he had come to Princeton to learn subtraction.

Although the main railroad lines originally passed through Princeton, when the route was straightened the main stop became Princeton Junction and the shuttle came into being in 1867. In 1918, soon after Blair Hall was built, the station was moved further down University Place (then called Railroad Avenue), along with the smoke and soot that blew into the students' rooms. Today the shuttle is generally known as "the Dinky."

Alexander Hall, designed by William Potter and built in 1892. Its Romanesque design represents one of the last major undertakings by the trustees before they adopted the Tudor Gothic style. From 1892 until 1922 all graduation exercises were held here. Now the hall with its newly renovated Richardson Auditorium is used for concerts, lectures, and political gatherings.

The building and the hall are named for three generations of Alexanders, all of whom had been trustees, and two generations of Richardsons.

153

Opposite, top: A snowy stroll down the campus past Whig Hall and Murray Dodge Hall.

Opposite, bottom: Dodge Gateway between Henry and 1901 Halls, given in 1933 by the parents of Marcellus Hartley Dodge, Jr., class of 1930. The lower campus is beautiful at any time of the year but a fresh snowfall makes it extraordinary.

Above: East Pyne, 1897, from the steps of Clio Hall. Originally Pyne Library, this building was designed by William Potter (who also designed Alexander Hall and Chancellor Green Library). In 1948, it became an administration building and is presently used for offices and classrooms.

Moses Taylor Pyne, class of 1877, gave more to Princeton than practically anyone else had given to any college. His grandfather, Moses Taylor, was the first president of the National City Bank in New York and a principal shareholder of the Delaware, Lackawanna and Western Railroad, which controlled New York's supply of coal. Pyne was married to Margaretta Stockton, a descendant of Richard Stockton, and lived in "Drumthwacket." Pyne was instrumental in organizing alumni support of the college and published in 1888 the first edition of the alumni directory. In 1900, he helped to develop a plan for the election of trustees and helped to found the *Alumni Weekly* and the body that became the Alumni Council.

Nassau Hall, 1756. Originally the largest building in America and capitol of the new United States in 1783. Over the years Nassau Hall has become synonymous with the college. Until its name was officially changed to Princeton University in 1896, many students referred to the college simply as Nassau Hall. Few other American colleges have been identified so completely and for so long a time with their first building.

During the Revolution, Nassau Hall was a military hospital and a barracks, and on January 3, 1777, it changed hands three times the same day.

Credit for raising the funds in England for its construction is due largely to Samuel Davies, fourth president of the college. In 1753 he sailed to England, a journey that took six weeks. His return trip was much worse, lasting three months, including a three-week layover in Plymouth because of bad weather (where he was confined to the small wooden ship). The fund-raising was successful. Davies spoke to congregations and wealthy individuals from London to Edinburgh. But the stormy trip back was extremely arduous. For two days, the captain admitted he was lost, and all of the passengers were sick. Davies was resigned to the very real probability the he would never see his family and would go down with the floundering ship. When Davies finally did arrive back in New York, a year and a half after his departure, there was no fanfare to meet him. Instead he had to hire a horse and, in spite of his fatigue, make the journey back to Princeton alone. There were not even coaches then.

The next time you walk past Nassau Hall you might think of the man who sailed across the ocean over two hundred years ago to raise the money for its construction and was prepared to give up his life in the process.

West College, built in 1836 and probably designed by John Notman, who later assisted in the renovation of Nassau Hall and the expansion of its prayer room in 1855. West College was Princeton's second dormitory after East College, which was removed to permit construction of the Pyne Library. It is now used for admissions and other administrative offices.

Behind Nassau Hall stood four buildings of similar design and construction, including the warm yellow ochre stone that is used in Nassau Hall: West and East College and Reunion and Philosophical Halls. Reunion was next to West College and was used as a dormitory; one of its freshman students was John F. Kennedy before he withdrew and transferred to Harvard. Philosophical Hall, also removed with East College during the construction of Pyne Library, housed the laboratory of Professor Joseph Henry, the college's (and indeed the nation's) premier scientist. Henry sent messages on wires from his office to his home telling his wife when he would be home for lunch. These short orders incorporated a magnetic relay which opened the way for the perfection of the telegraph, on which Henry collaborated with Samuel Morse.

Whig Hall, built 1837-1838 after a temple on the Island of Teos. Together with its twin, Clio Hall, these were the homes of the American Whig Society (founded in 1769) and the Cliosophic Society (founded in 1770), *the oldest college literary and debating clubs in the United States*. During the nineteenth century, these were the focus of undergraduate life. Their own libraries were larger than that of the college and they became in effect colleges within the college. The societies merged in 1928, and the combined operations are now located in Whig Hall.

When Whig-Clio extended a controversial speaking invitation to Alger Hiss in 1956, President Dodds made this comment: *One important element in education for human freedom is the freedom to make mistakes and to learn to accept responsibility for them. I've never believed in education without tears, even when the tears must be shared by the teacher.*

Over the past two hundred years Whig-Clio alumni have gone on to become federal and state supreme court justices (100), U.S. Representatives (200), college presidents (100), senators (65), and U.S. presidents (2).

Opposite, *top*: Chancellor Green Student Center, designed in 1873 by William Potter, who also designed Alexander Hall. This is pure Ruskinian Gothic, patterned after the Venetian Gothic style popularized in England by John Ruskin. This octagonal structure was Princeton's first separate library building and was given by John Green in memory of his brother Henry Woodhall Green, class of 1820 and Chancellor of New Jersey in the 1860s. While earlier buildings had been designed in the Georgian style, Chancellor Green's building altered the formal symmetry of the campus and signaled the change to what became predominantly Collegiate Gothic until the late 1940s. Chancellor Green facilities were soon outgrown and Pyne Library was built in 1897. Both were used as the university's library until Firestone Library was constructed in 1947.

Above: The interior of Chancellor Green Student Center. John Cleve Green, who gave the building in honor of his brother, was the greatest benefactor of the college during McCosh's presidency, even though he never attended the college. He was a member of the first class at Lawrenceville School but skipped college and went to New York and worked for foreign trade merchants. He was a principal benefactor of the Lawrenceville School, the Princeton Theological Seminary, and the college.

Opposite, *bottom*: Stanhope Hall, built in 1803 and named in 1915 in honor of William Stanhope Smith, the first graduate of the college to become its president (1795–1812). Under his administration the salary of the president was to be drawn in U.S. currency: fifteen hundred dollars per year. Stanhope Hall has also been known as the Library, Geological Hall, and the College Offices. It presently houses communications, publications, security, and other administrative offices.

McCosh Hall, built in 1906 (*above*) and Dickinson Hall, built in 1930 (*opposite, top*). McCosh has four large lecture rooms, fourteen recitation rooms, and twenty-six rooms especially designed for the small conferences (preceptorials) introduced by Woodrow Wilson in 1905. When it opened, McCosh Hall was the largest building on campus. James McCosh was the eleventh president of the college. He came to the United States from Scotland in 1866 and to Princeton in 1868. He played a significant role in helping to restore the college's faculty, enrollment, finances, and buildings after the Civil War.

Dickinson Hall was built in 1930 and is the home of the departments of economics and history. It is named for John Dickinson, first president of the college. He was a Presbyterian minister and a member of the fifth graduating class (1706) from the Collegiate School of Connecticut, later known as Yale College. His library was the college's and the parlor in his home was its first classroom.

Left: Campbell-Joline Arch. Campbell Hall was built in 1909, designed by Cram, Goodhue and Ferguson and presented to the university by the class of 1877. It is named for John Campbell who was class president during all four years in college and for fifty more thereafter. Pledges for the building came during a high-spirited dinner at the class's thirtieth reunion dinner in 1907.

Joline Hall was designed by Charles Klauder in 1932. It was a gift of the widow of Adrian H. Joline, class of 1870. Both Campbell and Joline are dormitories in the newly named Mathey College.

163

Above: The Rothschild Arch, connecting Dickinson Hall with the University Chapel, given in 1930 in memory of members of the Rothschild family.

Opposite: Pyne Hall archway. This is one of the university's largest dormitories and the first to house undergraduate women in 1969. It was designed by Day and Klauder in 1922 and given by the alumni in memory of Moses Taylor Pyne, class of 1877, one of the university's most generous benefactors. Pyne took a strong interest in developing the distinctive Collegiate Gothic building style on campus, helped finance Woodrow Wilson's preceptorial system, supported the development of a residential graduate college, and built Upper and Lower Pyne dormitories on Nassau Street as well as Pyne Library.

When he died in 1921 both the town and the university proclaimed a day of mourning. The shops were closed and classes suspended.

The interior courtyard of Pyne Hall (*opposite*) and magnolias near the school of architecture (*above*). Magnolias herald spring at what has been called "the most northern of the southern universities." There are approximately 160 magnolias of different varieties on the main campus ranging from white to red and many shades of pink. Many trees were introduced under the supervision of James Clark from 1930 to 1969. A recent survey recorded over two thousand trees on the central campus, representing 140 species.

I step out of a building and a sense of beauty washes over me: a visible reminder of the thoughtfulness and caring that have gone into building and maintaining Princeton. I suspect the buildings and trees of a campus give messages, suggesting the kind of place it is, whether it is and has been cherished. The messages are not explicit, but they're there. And students seem to understand them.

—Joan S. Girgus, Dean of the College

167

Above: Forbes College, designed in 1924 by Andrew Thomas. For many years it was known as the Princeton Inn, a familiar landmark because of its gracious design and setting, with a large veranda overlooking a pond, the Springdale golf course, and the graduate college. The university converted the inn into its first co-educational dormitory in 1970 to meet a housing shortage. In 1985, the inn was renamed Forbes College in honor of Malcolm Stevenson Forbes, father class of 1941 and son class of 1970.

Opposite: The magnolias of Blair Hall, built in 1897, and Spelman Hall, designed by I.M. Pei and built in 1973. Laura Spelman Rockefeller, with her husband John D., Sr., founded Spelman College in Atlanta, the first American college for black women. Their grandson, Laurance S. Rockefeller, class of 1932, gave four million dollars to Princeton in 1969 to help institute co-education. Spelman Hall is the first to have an apartment design with individual kitchens, and living and dining areas.

168

169

The lower campus of the university. Laughlin Hall (*left*), designed by Day and Klauder in 1926 and given by James Laughlin, class of 1868, who also gave the large tract of land on which the majority of the playing fields are now located.

Class of 1904—Howard Henry Memorial Dormitory (*right*), also known as Henry Hall. It was designed by Zantzinger, Borie and Medary in 1923 and given by the class of 1904 as well as the family and friends of two classmates, Howard Henry and Samuel Pyne, both killed in World War I.

The beauty of the setting, the trees, the space, is to be savored. They provide the serenity and refreshment of soul so important to learning and thinking. Of course, if setting were all Princeton offered, I wouldn't be here, because I

like the intensity of a city But Princeton provides marked contrasts: between its small size and great stature; its bucolic location and sophisticated architecture; its tranquil air and feverish intellectual activity; between its conservative past and its liberal present. In fact these contrasts may be what most clearly distinguish Princeton from similar universities.

—Natalie Z. Davis,
Professor of History

Above: The cloister of Holder Hall, now part of Rockefeller College. This was a gift of Margaret Sage, widow of Russell Sage, in honor of Christopher Holder, a member of the Society of Friends in the seventeenth century.

Opposite: The upper campus at sunset showing Campbell and Joline Halls, part of Mathey College. Dean Mathey, class of 1912, was a successful investment banker, an alumni trustee, a donor of faculty housing near the graduate college, and co-donor of the tennis pavilion.

The use of the word *campus* (Latin for "field") to mean the grounds of a college originated at Princeton. Its earliest recorded date was 1774 and its originator was probably President John Witherspoon, who, accustomed to the city universities of Scotland, must have been struck by the different aspect at Princeton, where the college grounds consisted of a perfectly flat field with no enclosures; he was therefore moved to apply to the grounds "a classical term which fitly described their character."

Previously *yard* was the word used at Princeton, and the two were used interchangeably until 1833 when *campus* won out over *yard*.

Opposite: Hamilton Hall, designed by Day and Klauder in 1911 and part of Mathey College. This is one of the smallest Gothic dormitories and perhaps the most charming. It was a gift of members of the classes of 1884 and 1885 and named for John Hamilton, acting governor of the Province of New Jersey, who granted the first charter to the College of New Jersey on October 22, 1746. Hamilton acted against the precedent of the governor he succeeded and, more unusual, gave the charter to a board of trustees who were entirely Presbyterian, in spite of the fact that he was an Episco-palian. This was at a time when Episcopalian governors were not in favor of granting to the Presbyterians any ecclesiastical or educational franchises.

Above: Brown Hall, designed by John Lyman Faxon in 1892 after a Florentine palace and one of the university's last experiments in architectural variations before adopting the Collegiate Gothic style. The dormitory was given by Mrs. David B. Brown in memory of her husband. She also gave Dod Hall in memory of her brother, mathematics professor Albert B. Dod.

McCormick Hall, designed in 1922 by Ralph Adams Cram in Siennese Gothic. It was a gift of Cyrus McCormick, class of 1879, and his family. It is the home of the department of art and archeology, the Marquand Library, and, until 1963, the school of architecture.

Allan Marquand, class of 1874, was the son of a New York banker and a co-founder of the Metropolitan Museum of Art. He founded the department of art and archeology at Princeton and, together with Charles Eliot Norton of Harvard, is credited with being the first to introduce the serious study of art into the American college curriculum.

Fine Hall, designed in 1968 by Warner, Burns, Toan and Lunde and named in honor of Henry Burchard Fine, first dean of the department of science. Fine was a member of the class of 1880 and did the most in helping Princeton to develop from a college into a university. He also made Princeton the leading center for mathematical study and he fostered the growth of creative work in other branches of science.

Upon completion of this building, the original Fine Hall was renamed Jones Hall in honor of Thomas D. Jones, class of 1876, who was a close friend of Fine's and Woodrow Wilson's.

Blair Hall (*above*) and Nassau Hall and Cannon Green (*opposite*). Cannon Green is the site of "Big Cannon" which was left in Princeton after the Revolution. In 1812, it was transported to New Brunswick to defend that city from a possible enemy attack. It was recaptured in 1836 by a group of Princeton citizens and students that included Winston Churchill's grandfather and was buried in its present location, muzzle down, in 1840.

Princeton wouldn't have the emanations it has without two and a half centuries behind it: the history that's taken place here, and the concept of the university sustained throughout all that.

Princeton's presence is formidable and inescapable. From the beginning, you powerfully identify with it or resist it, love it or hate it; you can't ignore it. This is one source of Princeton's energy, and of its ability to communicate its energy: the way it refuses to take "no" for an answer. Even if you don't like it, you have to end up with a positive feeling for what human attention, care, and loving concern have created over many generations. The residential nature of the university, the total environment—there is no alternative to finding one's place in it. And yet it is open enough, large enough, varied enough not to be felt as constricting. It is now, after all, a community of some ten thousand people, students, faculty, and staff.

—Neil L. Rudenstein, Provost of the University

Seventy-Nine Hall, built in 1904 and given by the 170 members of the class of 1879 at their twenty-fifth reunion to Princeton and to their own classmate, Woodrow Wilson. When Wilson was president of the university he had his office here. Originally the building was a dormitory, whose rooms were highly coveted by upperclassmen because of their proximity to the eating clubs. Now it is used for academic purposes. The style is the same Tudor Gothic employed by Blair and Little Halls, although red brick has been used instead of gray stone. The vaulted archway is a popular spot for singing groups, and it is familiar to all returning alumni who march in the June P-Rade.

The namesake of the famous 1879 classmate is the Woodrow Wilson School of Public and International Affairs, founded in 1930. Harold W. Dodds, its first chairman, later became president of the university and served from 1933 to 1947. In 1980 he said, *It is a notorious fact that America attracts to public service too small a proportion of the best capacity of the nation. In no field is the divorce of education and daily life so striking as in politics and public administration. For one hundred years we have slumbered in a peaceful trust that free government is the ultimate remedy of our social ills. Suddenly we awake to the instability of cherished institutions...The time is fast due for a return to the earlier relationship of education and the state, by integrating our colleges and universities with public service in government and business.*

Today the admissions office believes that part of Princeton's mission is to educate students who are going to make a contribution to their communities when they graduate.

Opposite, top: The Woodrow Wilson School of Public and International Affairs. This magnificent building with fifty-eight quartz columns was designed by Minoru Yamasaki in 1966. It was made possible by a large gift of Charles Robertson, class of 1926, and his wife, and it was dedicated in 1966 with addresses by university president Robert F. Goheen and President Lyndon B. Johnson.

The Woodrow Wilson School was founded in 1930 as a cooperative enterprise of the departments of history, politics and economics. In 1948, it was officially named, and a graduate program was established. The school is designed to prepare students for careers in public service.

Opposite, bottom: The Woolworth Center of Musical Studies, built in 1963 and largely a gift of Frasier McCann, class of 1930, and his sister in memory of their grandfather, F.W. Woolworth. At the left in the photograph may be seen the edge of Palmer Hall, built in 1909 as a gift of Stephen Palmer, a trustee. It formerly housed the department of physics. Presently it houses various programs including the Princeton-in-Asia program, the History of Science, and Women's Studies.

Above: The view between McCosh and Dickinson Halls looking past the school of architecture building and the Woolworth Center and towards Palmer Hall. A mixture of modern and Tudor Gothic has been blended into a harmonious quadrangle with the common use of red brick and limestone.

Opposite, top: Gordon Wu Hall, designed by Robert Venturi in 1984 and given by Mr. Wu, class of 1958. This dining and social center is part of Butler College, one of the university's five residential colleges. It won the honor award of the American Institute of Architects in 1984.

Opposite, bottom: The Thompson Courtyard of East Pyne. Henry B. Thompson, class of 1877, probably had more influence on the physical appearance of Princeton during the period of unprecedented expansion from 1909 to 1928 than any other person. As a trustee and chairman of its committee on grounds and buildings, he oversaw construction of twenty-five campus buildings beginning with Holder Hall and ending with the University Chapel.

Above: The new Lewis Thomas Laboratory, designed by Robert Venturi in 1985 and made possible by a gift of Laurance Rockefeller, class of 1932. Over $46 million has been reserved for the study of molecular biology (biochemistry and genetics), and the $29 million cost of the laboratory building represents the university's most expensive structure to date. Lewis Thomas, for whom the laboratory is named, is a member of the class of 1933 and is a noted research physician.

Stafford Little Hall, built in 1899, with an extension in 1901, designed by Cope and Stewardson. This was Princeton's second Collegiate Gothic building after Blair Hall, also designed by the same Philadelphia firm. It is named for Stafford Little, class of 1844, founder of the New York and Long Branch Railroad. Together with Blair Hall, these dormitories set the tone for the architectural style on the Princeton campus for fifty years and influenced other American college campuses as well.

Lockhart Hall, designed in 1927 by Charles Klauder, whose firm was largly responsible for many of the upperclass dormitories. This was a gift of James H. Lockhart, class of 1887. The combination of the mag- nolia tree at the edge of Blair Hall and the lights in the windows adds a romantic touch to a beautiful section of the campus.

Holder Hall, designed in 1909 by Day and Klauder. This was a gift of Margaret Sage, widow of Russell Sage, in honor of their ancestor, Christopher Holder, a member of the Society of Friends in the seventeenth century. Ralph Adams Cram said the architects reached their highest point in authoritative interpretation of Gothic as a living style with this building complex.

Holder is now the principal residence of Rockefeller College which includes Madison, Witherspoon, and part of Blair Hall. It is named for John D. Rockefeller III and Laurance S. Rockefeller, classes of 1929 and 1932 respectively. All freshmen and sophomores live in five residential colleges, each with 450 to 500 members: Woodrow Wilson, Forbes (formerly Princeton Inn), Rockefeller, Mathey (encompassing Blair, Camp-

bell, Hamilton, and Joline Halls), and Butler (encompassing Patton, Lourie-Love, and Dormitories of the Classes of 1915, 1922, 1940, 1941, and 1942).

Princeton's residential life is a direct expression of a concept of liberal education that seeks to develop all of a student's capacities—including the capacities to learn, to live a full life, and to serve others. It assumes that the transactions of the classroom, library, and laboratory, important as they are, should be complemented by the experience of living with fellow students of many backgrounds and persuasions and participating actively with faculty members and students in the life of an academic community.

—William G. Bowen,
President of the University

189

Cuyler Hall (*above*) and 1903 Hall (*opposite, top*), two upperclass dormitories designed by the Klauder firm in 1912 and 1929 respectively. Cornelius Cuyler was a classmate and friend of Woodrow Wilson's, a New York banker, and a trustee of the university from 1898 to 1909. This is considered one of the handsomest dormitories.

Walker Memorial Dormitory (*opposite, bottom*), designed in 1929 also by Charles Klauder and given by members of the Walker family in honor of James T. Walker, class of 1927. This dormitory is part of Woodrow Wilson College, which encompasses Wilcox, Dodge-Osborn, Gauss, part of Patton, and the Dormitories of the Classes of 1937, 1938, and 1939.

The pond on the Springdale Golf Course reflecting the graduate college (*above*) and Forbes College (*right*).

Woodrow Wilson originally proposed a plan of quadrangles or colleges in 1906, patterned after Oxford. One of his reasons was to diminish the influence the eating clubs were having on the undergraduates. The residential college system has now been implemented in order to invigorate residential life at Princeton, and a way to create a sense of community while encompassing a diverse student population.

Students will do better for themselves, and for society, if at every stage from prekindergarten to postdoctural study their creative and critical abilities are encouraged and nourished; if instead of being spoon-fed they are required to think for themselves. It's Princeton's policy to treat every student this way, although obviously not all are equally creative and critical. Other universities have honor programs in which a few students are so treated; at Princeton every student is.

—Robert F. Goheen, class of 1940
President of the University, 1957 to 1972

Princeton's two most outstanding buildings, the University Chapel, built between 1925 and 1928 (*left*), and Firestone Library, built in 1947 (*above*).

The University Chapel is said to be one of the most beautiful Gothic buildings in America, and it is the third largest college church in the world. It contains no steel but rather was built in the same manner as the original Gothic cathedrals. It was designed by Ralph Adams Cram who also designed St. Thomas' and the Cathedral of St. John the Divine, both in New York. Cram became the university's supervising architect from 1907 to 1929, and more than any other person shaped the appearance of the campus with his famed Collegiate Gothic style. Princeton's Gothic was to be dramatic and exciting, with a different view at every turn, containing a literary interest and culminating with Cram's greatest achievement, the chapel.

The Firestone Library, a gift in honor of Harvey S. Firestone by his five alumni sons, is the largest open-stack research library in the world. In order that the chapel retain its prominence on the campus, the trustees suggested that the library not be any taller. Instead, it extends substantially underground, into the foreground of the photograph as well as to the rear, where a sloping terrain and garden wells provide adequate lighting. Only about 15 percent of the library facilities are thus visible from this viewpoint.

Above: Murray-Dodge Hall, built in 1879 and 1900, respectively, with funds provided by Hamilton Murray, class of 1872, and the Dodge family in memory of Earl Dodge, class of 1879. Dodge Hall (on the *right*) is the center of religious activities and Murray Hall (on the *left*) is the home of Theatre Intime and other drama groups.

Opposite, top and bottom: Firestone Library, symbolic of Princeton's emphasis on independent research, study, and writing. Princeton has the highest per-student circulation of any university library in the United States (possibly in the world): presently 113 books per student per year.

197

Students reading in Firestone Library (*above*) and Jones Library (*opposite*). Firestone has fifty-five miles of open shelving, three million seven hundred thousand books and journals, approximately ten million manuscript items, plus an additional four million microforms, maps, and prints. It contains several thousand study seats and over five hundred closed study carrels.

Jones Hall was renamed when the new Fine Hall was completed in honor of one of the latter's original donors, Thomas D. Jones, class of 1876. It houses the departments of East Asian studies and Near Eastern studies. Until the Institute for Advanced Study's main building, Fuld Hall, was completed in 1939, Albert Einstein's office was located here.

Firestone Library. The Scribner Rooms (*opposite, top*) are named in memory of five generations of Scribners who founded the publishing firm and bookstore in New York and the Princeton University Press (and donated its first building), co-founded the *Princeton Alumni Weekly,* and donated over 250,000 books and other documents to the university in 1967.

Harold W. Dodds, the university's fifteenth president, began work on the new library in 1933 because of his commitment to the education of the broad reaches of the mind. At the laying of the cornerstone in 1947, he said, *Within the walls of this building the miracle will constantly occur that we take for granted, because the process is quiet and continuous rather than spectacular and instantaneous; the miracle of the imagination kindled, preju-* *dice thrown overboard, dogma rejected, conviction strengthened, perspective lengthened. This miracle is performed by teachers and students together through the instrumentality of books.*

The main reading room (*opposite, bottom*). Princeton's trustees voted to admit women in 1969 because they concluded that the educational experience would be improved when carried out in mixed rather than single-sex circumstances. Today admission is without consideration of sex, and women constitute approximately 38 percent of the undergraduate student body. The university had originally considered coeducation in 1887 with the founding of Evelyn College (which closed its doors ten years later in part because of financial setbacks during the panic of 1893).

Reading and reminiscing in the Chancellor Green Student Center, the old library (*opposite, top*), and Firestone Library (*opposite, bottom*). Ira Wade (*above*) received one of the first graduate degrees in Romance languages from Princeton in 1924 and was chairman of the department of Romance languages and literatures from 1946 to 1958.

This is a place where students and faculty get to know each other, and if I had to choose the one aspect of Princeton that most clearly distinguishes it, that would be it: The way the learners and teachers relate to each other. There are, of course, other universities where individual scholars and scientists are dedicated to teaching undergraduates, but those individuals tend to be exceptions. The concept of scholar-teacher is better realized here than at any other place I know of.

Because of the faculty's accessibility, students frequently acquire an unusual attitude toward learning: some of their professors' enthusiasm for the material rubs off on them. They discover learning can be fun—serious fun, but fun. And they get enthusiastic about the give-and-take of teaching and learning. A kind of union develops between professor and students, a sense of common purpose.

—Carlos Baker,
Chairman Emeritus of the Department of English

Firestone is the central library on the campus with all volumes in the various university collections being centered here. It is actively used by undergraduates, graduate students, professors and friends.

Knowledge will forever govern ignorance: And a people who mean to be their own governors must arm themselves with the power which knowledge gives.
—James Madison, class of 1771
(the father of the Constitution)

Reading in Frick Chemical Library (*opposite*) and Firestone (*left*). The Frick Chemical Laboratory was donated by Henry Clay Frick, a Pittsburgh steelmaker, who originally had thought of helping to establish a law school. President Hibben persuaded him to donate a chemical laboratory instead.

One of Firestone's five hundred study carrels (*below*), available to seniors and graduate students writing theses in the humanities and social sciences. The word *carrel* comes from the Middle English for carole, a round dance or ring. It is generally meant to be a table with bookshelves, often enclosed. Carrels are conducive to individual study in a library.

An exam in McCosh 50 under the honor system.

We have placed our hopes on the understanding of our people. It is a magnificent gamble. And it is to education, the universities, to Princeton, that we look for so very much. How well it does its job determines how each generation resolves that magnificent gamble, for it involves the idea of freedom and the search for truth. We can have no higher hope or aspiration for Princeton, but that it will do it well.
—Adlai Stevenson, class of 1922

The Honor System and the Preceptorial Method

Both of these unusual systems were introduced to Princeton University under Woodrow Wilson's presidency at the turn of the century. The honor system originated in 1893 due to student dissatisfaction with faculty proctoring of exams. Princeton was the third American college to have an honor system, after the College of William & Mary and the University of Virginia, and it remains largely unchanged today. Each examination paper bears the signed pledge, substantially in its original form:

> I pledge my honor
> that during this examination
> I have neither given nor received assistance.

The students accept full responsibility for their conduct in written examinations. There is no proctoring and the honor code is enforced by a committee of students. The basic tenet is less a rule than a state of mind: that honesty in examinations is assured. As William Hudnut, class of 1927, recently said, "In an age that is all too possessed with the bottom line and all too eager for the short cut, Princeton has provided us with a noble heritage—a tradition of integrity and honorable dealing."

The preceptorial method was introduced by Woodrow Wilson in 1905. It was his idea, concept and name, loosely patterned on the Oxford tutorial. He wanted to replace the old-fashioned recitation method and give the undergraduates "their proper release from being school boys." The basic concept is a group tutorial with preceptors, using the Socratic method of instruction by questioning. Juniors are assigned a preceptor who guides them in all reading and work in the department. The more gifted students are encouraged to read independently and to be excused from the ordinary weekly classes. Wilson wanted to bring the methods and personal contact between teacher and pupil, which are characteristic of the small college, into a great university. When it was first introduced, the comments by the students and the press were favorable, and the American educational world watched with great interest. When McCosh Hall was built in 1906, it was the largest building on the campus and it contained twenty-six rooms especially designed for preceptorial conferences.

The magnificent ceiling of the Chancellor Green Student Center (*above*) and the Pitney archway of Cuyler Hall (*opposite*). The archway was installed in 1921 in honor of the Pitney family and represents Day and Klauder's finest achievement in the Gothic vaulted arch.

There are nine shields or class numerals in this magnificent vault, including the initials of Henry Cooper Pitney in the center (he was class of 1848 and vice-chancellor of the State of New Jersey), O.H. Pitney, class of 1881 and university trustee, Henry C. Pitney, class of 1877 and Mahlon Pitney, class of 1879 and supreme court justice. Mahlon Pitney and Cornelius Cuyler, who gave the dormitory, were classmates.

The seal of the College of New Jersey appears at the lower right of center and of Princeton University at the upper left.

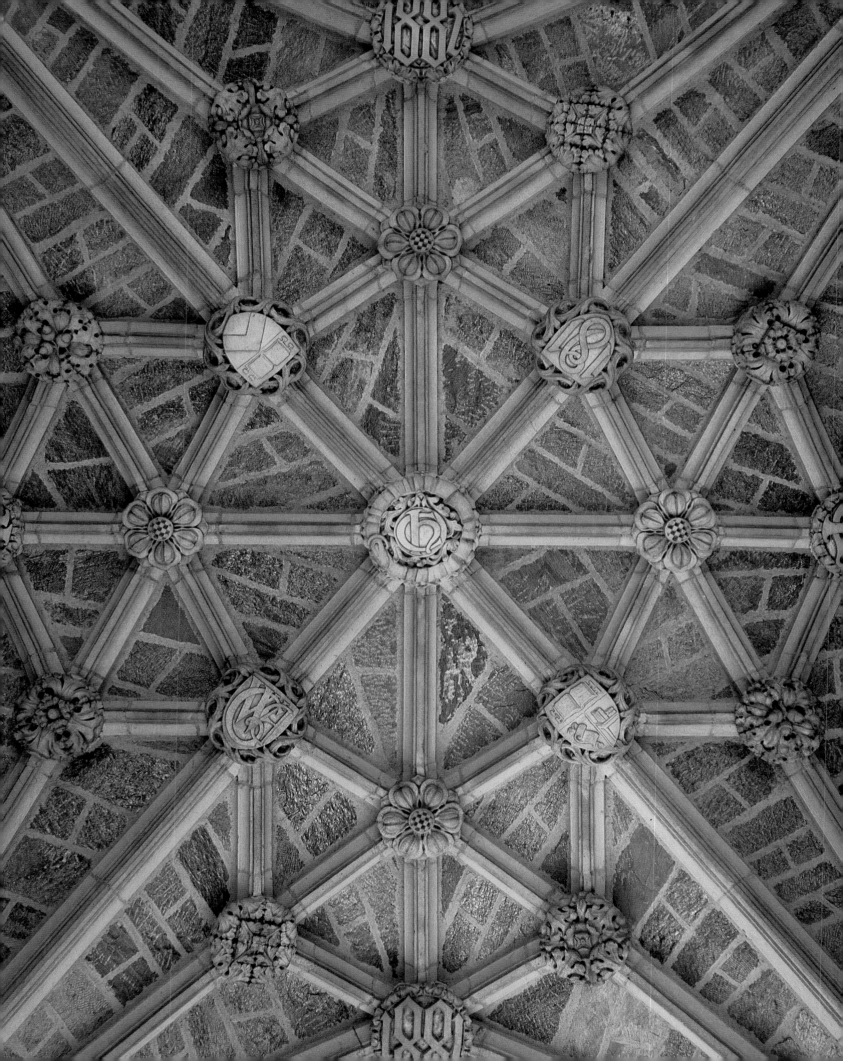

The great tympanum over the main entrance to the University Chapel. This is the "majesty of Jesus Christ" as described by St. John in *Revelations*. He is seated and supported by two angels and wearing the golden crown. The four animals are the symbols of the Evangelists: lion—Mark, angel—Matthew, eagle—John, ox—Luke.

O Eternal God, the source of life and light for all peoples, we pray that you would endow this University with your grace and wisdom. Give inspiration to those who teach and understanding to those who learn. Grant vision to its trustees and administrators. And to all who work here and to all its graduates the world wide give your guiding Spirit of sacrificial courage and loving service. Amen.

—A prayer for Princeton

An Alexander Hall frieze, sculpted by J. Massey Rhind in 1892. The group represents the arts and sciences paying tribute to learning, the central figure. Left of learning are figures representing language and theology. To the right of learning are art, sculpture, and painting. Each figure holds a symbol of the represented art.

Left: One of the "arts windows" in the University Chapel. In this window *medicine* is represented by the Persian physician, Al-Rasi, who holds a scroll containing his treatise on medicine.

Opposite: The great north window: Christ the Martyr. The theme of this window, one of the four largest in the chapel, is stated in the text carved in the stone beneath: *He that shall endure unto the end, the same shall be saved* (Mark 13:13).

Christ is the central figure of the window. He is clad in the martyr's red and wears the crown of thorns. To his right and left are the archangels Gabriel and Raphael. Beneath the figure of Christ is Michael, clad in armor and holding a flaming sword. The panel just below represents him weighing the souls. In the small panels below are shown the Flagellation of Christ, Christ Crowned with Thorns, and Christ Carrying the Cross. In the pair of lancets to the left of Gabriel are St. Sebastian, and St. Stephen, first martyr. In the pair of lancets to the right are St. Lawrence, and St. Christopher, carrying the Infant Christ. In the panel beneath he carries the fully grown Christ, and thus the sins of the world.

214

Above: One of the university's many music groups, giving a performance in the chapel.

Without yielding one step of our position as to the place of intellectual development in the university's scheme of things, Princeton, as a residential college, seeks to offer opportunities for spiritual and physical development as well. In keeping with its interest in the whole person, the university recognizes that it must offer opportunities for fun—for the natural expression of human instincts in leisure time.

—Harold W. Dodds,
President of the University, 1933 to 1957

Opposite: The windows on the north side of the University Chapel nave depict scenes from the Old and New Testaments. The late afternoon sun transforms the chapel into a multihued temple. The chapel can seat eighteen hundred people but is well proportioned so as not to appear oversized.

Be thou my Vision, O Lord of my heart;
Naught be all else to me, save that thou art—
Thou my best thought, by day or by night,
Waking or sleeping, thy presence my light.

—an old Irish hymn

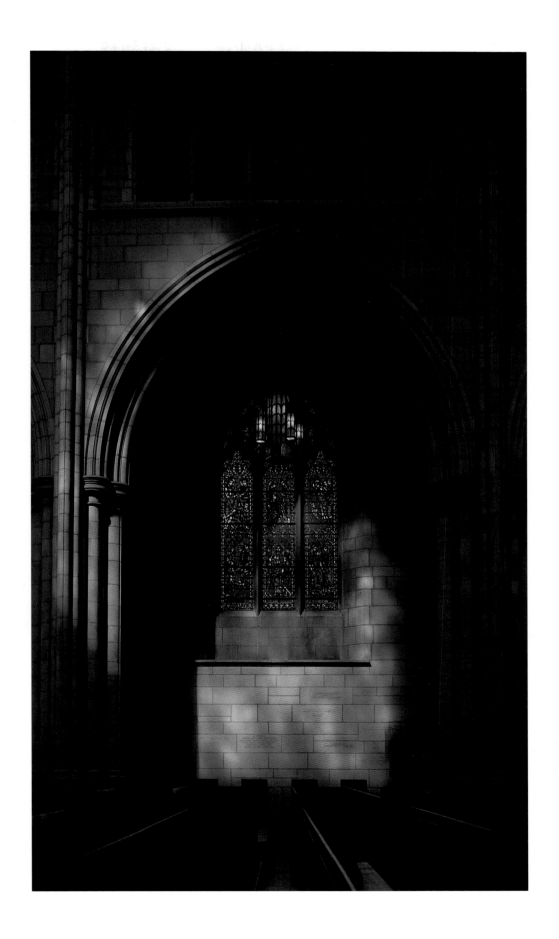

217

The University Chapel choir, before a Sunday service (*above*) and marching around the chapel on Palm Sunday (*opposite*). With their assistance, the congregation has come a long way from 1774 when John Adams, later President of the United States, reported that the scholars in Princeton sang as badly as the Presbyterians in New York.

Today the chapel is open every day from 8:00 A.M. until 12:30 A.M. The facilities are available to all denominated societies, of which there are presently eleven: Episcopal, Presbyterian, Catholic, Methodist, Evangelical, Jewish, Lutheran, Baptist, Unitarian, Christian Science, and Greek Orthodox.

How do we find grounds for hope and faith, for courage and compassion in our lives? How do we form our values and stick to them when times are tough? How may we experience God who is so visibly absent but yet mysteriously present in our world? Many students and faculty ask these questions and want to explore the possibilities for love, for building communities, and for service in a world often rent by heartbreak and tragedy. Those of us who minister on campus try to help them and share with them in that exploration.

—Frederick Borsch, Dean of the Chapel

Above: Stone carvings on East Pyne. *Opposite, left:* John Witherspoon, signer of the Declaration of Independence and president of the college from 1768 to 1794. *Opposite, right:* James McCosh, president of the college from 1868 to 1888.

These two Presbyterian ministers from Scotland ran Princeton for a total of almost fifty years and each helped to steer the college onto firmer ground and onto becoming the great university it is today. Witherspoon broadened the curriculum, faculty, and overall support of the college and, equally important, held it together during the destructive years of the Revolution. McCosh arrived a hundred years after Witherspoon and was faced with a similar restoration challenge, this time following the withdrawal of many students during the Civil War. To this day Princeton is regarded as a southern school; in the 1850s over a third of the student body came from the South. McCosh was able to build back the enrollment after the war and add to the college's curriculum, endowment and facilities. Under his leadership the Chancellor Green Library was built, containing an unprecedented 70,000 volumes.

He was also concerned about the landscaping of the campus and was a familiar figure on "McCosh Walk." His wife, Isabella, took an interest in those students who were sick, caring for them and writing their families, and ultimately in 1891 persuaded the trustees to build an infirmary. Both the first such facility and its replacement in 1925 were named for her.

221

Above: Tigers on Joline-Campbell arch and Foulke Hall. *Opposite, top:* Whimsical gargoyles on the campus.

Originally gargoyles were grotesque figures serving as water spouts on the great cathedrals in Europe (*gargoyle* derives from an old French word meaning "mouth"). Princeton brought the stone genre form back into popularity when it built so many of its buildings in the Collegiate Gothic style. The students studying or listening to a wind-up Victrola are on the side of the North Court of the graduate college—built in the high-spirited 1920s.

The pensive student and football player in quilted pants and a stocking cap adorn Dickinson and McCosh Halls, respectively. The dress of the player is reflective of the period when McCosh was built: 1906. At the time of its dedication McCosh was the largest building on campus.

Princeton football players of the 1920s, on Dillon Gymnasium (*opposite*), Henry Hall (*right*), and Foulke Hall (*above*). Leather helmets were popular then. Although Dillon Gymnasium was constructed in 1947, its principal donor, Herbert Dillon, was a member of the class of 1907 and the style is reflective of the period.

Opposite, top: Head of a Woman by Pablo Picasso, standing at the front entrance to the Art Museum. This concrete, stone, and iron sculpture was executed *in situ* for Princeton in 1971 by the Norwegian artist Carl Nesjar under the supervision of Picasso.

The Art Museum was established by Allan Marquand as a teaching museum. Its collection approximates the department's curriculum and ranges from ancient to contemporary. It includes pre-Columbian artifacts, Italian seventeenth-century paintings and drawings, a window from Chartres Cathedral, sculpture from the Sung Dynasty, and twentieth-century paintings and photographs.

Opposite, bottom: Song of the Vowels by Jacques Lipchitz. This is one of a series of sculptures by Lithuanian-born Lipchitz that was inspired by his obsession with the harp—originally the harpists at symphony concerts in Paris in the 1920s. This sculpture was executed in 1969 and stands in front of the Firestone Library.

Above: Oval with Points by Henry Moore. This bronze sculpture was completed in 1970 and within a few months of its installation (to the delight of the sculptor) the interior curves of the lower part of the oval had been burnished through contact with people sitting on or sliding through it.

The sculptures shown on these and the following pages are from the John B. Putnam Memorial Collection, named in honor of an alumnus killed in air combat in 1944. In his diary he had written on one of his last days, "Courage is not the lack of fear but the ability to face it."

Above: Upstart II by Clement Meadmore in front of the engineering quadrangle. This is a product of the minimalist movement, in which strict economy of means produces purity of image. The sculpture creates an impression of material lightness in spite of its size and weight. It aggressively elbows out the surrounding atmosphere as it makes its ascent, like a person who inhabits a place. Meadmore executed this sculpture in 1970.

The school of engineering was organized in 1921 as Princeton's second professional school, although engineering courses had been part of the curriculum since 1875. The engineering quadrangle was built in 1962 and contains 120 laboratories, twenty-five classrooms, a library, and a communication room, as well as more than 125 faculty offices and graduate study spaces.

Opposite, top: Five Disks: One Empty by Alexander Calder, located on the plaza between Fine and Jadwin Halls. This was designed for Princeton in 1969 and installed in 1971. Originally the disks were painted orange but the sculptor decided that the uniform black was best.

Opposite, bottom: Construction in the Third and Fourth Dimension by Antoine Pevsner, located in the courtyard of Jadwin Hall. Like many of Pevsner's sculptures, this one exploits the contortion of flat metal planes, capable of indefinite projection. The linear striations on the planes add to the tension and also suggest infinite continuity. This sculpture was executed in 1962 and installed in 1972.

Jadwin Hall since 1970 has been the headquarters of the physics department. It was designed by Hugh Stubbins & Associates and given, together with Fine Hall and Jadwin Gymnasium, by the Jadwin family in memory of L. Stockwell Jadwin, class of 1928.

To me there is a joy that runs through teaching, at three levels: the celebration, one, of what man has achieved in the past; two, of what the student before you has achieved; and three, of what you have achieved by getting the student to achieve.

But if teaching can be a joy, learning can be painful. Glorious, rewarding, exciting, yes! But not easy. Over and over to be put in the position of a fledgling; to be handed a hammer, then, as soon as you learn to use that, to have it snatched away and be handed a screwdriver.

—Aaron Lemonick,
Dean of the Faculty, Professor of Physics

Opposite: The Mather Sun Dial. This is a replica of the Turnball sun dial erected in 1551 at Corpus Christi College, Oxford. It was given in 1907 by Sir William Mather, governor of Victoria University in Manchester, England. Until the 1950s, this was the exclusive domain of Princeton University seniors. The pelican at the top is a religious symbol for Corpus Christi (body of Christ). Around the base is this inscription:

> *Loyalty is e'er the same*
> *whether it win or lose the game*
> *True as the dial to the sun*
> *Although it be not shined upon*

Above: Nassau Hall and the Adams Mall between Whig and Clio Halls. Two bronze figure tigers by Bruce Moore were installed in 1969. They are male and female in commemoration of Princeton's voting to become a co-educational university in 1969.

Although the class of 1879 had given a pair of bronze lions to grace the front steps of Nassau Hall, the tiger was becoming the official token of the university in the 1880s and 1890s. The football teams wore stockings and jerseys of orange and black stripes. The tiger appeared in Princeton songs in the 1880s and the university's humor magazine, published first in 1882, was called *The Tiger*. An eating club called the Inn became Tiger Inn in 1893 and finally the class of 1879 substituted its lions with bronze tigers by A.P. Proctor in 1911. The tiger symbol had become firmly established.

Cannon Green (*above*), McCosh Walk (*opposite, top*) and McCosh Hall (*opposite, bottom*). President and Mrs. McCosh took a personal interest in the landscaping of the campus, laying out paths, and in selecting sites for new buildings. They lived at "Prospect" and were familiar figures strolling along this walk named for them. Upon his retirement and moving out of "Prospect," McCosh said he felt like Adam leaving Eden.

233

Left: Rothschild Arch, given in 1930 by members of the Rothschild family.

Below: Jadwin Gymnasium, completed in 1969 and named for Leander Stockwell Jadwin, class of 1928, one of Princeton's greatest track stars. The field house was designed by Walker Cain & Associates and has more than enough total floor space to enclose *eight* football fields. It provides year-round facilities for competition and practice in ten sports as well as concerts and convocations. It can accommodate ten thousand spectators.

Peter Carril, one of Princeton's great coaches, advises his students, *The most important thing you can do is what you're doing when you're doing it. When you study, study and when you play, play. At Princeton, the players are smart. They understand you have to take advantage of your strong points, adapt to your environment. We don't have the big guys, the stars, so we have to make the best of what we have.* Concentration and playing smart are reasons why Princeton has such high athletic and academic standings in the Ivy League.

Opposite: Dillon Gymnasium, built in 1947 through the generosity of Herbert Lowell Dillon, class of 1907. The building is designed in the Gothic style and includes a famous football player as a gargoyle. During the period between 1963 and 1965 Princeton attained the highest level of excellence it had known in basketball, winning three successive league championships under the leadership of Bill Bradley, class of 1965 and now a U.S. Senator.

Predecessors of Dillon Gymnasium were University Gymnasium, built in 1903 and the largest in the country when it was completed, and Bonner Gymnasium built, in 1869 as the first large gymnasium built by any American college.

Opposite, top: Tennis was introduced as a sport at Princeton in 1882, soccer (*opposite, bottom*) in 1905, and rugby (*above*) in 1931. Women's soccer was introduced in 1969 when coeducation began.

Today the university has thirty-two varsity teams and twenty-five "club" teams. For the past five years, it has been at or near the top of the Ivy League composite standing in all sports. The phrase "Ivy League" was coined in the 1930s by a *New York Herald Tribune* sports writer as it applied to eight universities: Brown, Columbia, Cornell, Dartmouth, Harvard, Pennsylvania, Princeton, and Yale.

Princeton Athletics

The variety and depth of the athletic program at Princeton shows the commitment of the university to the whole education of the individual and the belief that a properly channeled outlet for physical activity enhances the capacity for intellectual pursuits. Princeton has achieved a number of athletic accomplishments equaled by few other institutions. The first game of football was played in 1869 between Princeton and Rutgers. Princeton has been invited to play in the Rose Bowl and in 1922 went to Chicago for what was the Super Bowl of its time and the first football game in history to be broadcast.

Less known are some of Princeton's other significant accomplishments: participation in the first intercollegiate basketball game and the first collegiate track contest, and the largest number of Americans for the first modern Olympics in 1896—at which Princetonians won more olive branches than any other national contingent. Today Princeton is at the top of the Ivy League in the composite standing of all sports and has one of the largest percentages of participating students of any institution its size. The university has thirty-two varsity teams (including fourteen women's teams) plus twenty-five "club" teams.

But athletics were not always favored. They were a development initially encouraged by James McCosh, who introduced a more liberal attitude toward sports and built the first large gymnasium at any American college in 1869.

In the early years under John Witherspoon, students were not allowed to leave their rooms without permission except for a half hour after morning prayer, an hour and a half after dinner, and from evening prayers until seven o'clock. Furthermore, none of the students were permitted to play cards or dice, for which there was a fine for the first two offenses and expulsion for the third. And there was to be "no jumping, hollering or boisterous noise" in the college at any time. Nevertheless, the more restrictive the regulations, the more desirous the students were to break them. Hazing and sprees were popular, including an occasional horse race in Nassau Hall's upper corridors. Horn sprees were also popular. The first one occurred when a large number of horns were present to supplement the "rouser" who was charged with blowing a horn at 5:00 to awaken students for prayers. Later that evening horns were blown on the top story of Nassau Hall, and when the tutors rushed up the horns were tossed out the windows to accomplices outside, who brought them up one stairway while the tutors rushed back down another. The horn sprees continued in one form or another for about fifty years.

Opposite: Lacrosse with Dartmouth, during and after the match. This game originated among the American Indians and was developed by the French in Canada. Harvard, Columbia and New York University took up the game in 1880, Princeton in 1881 and Yale the following year.

239

Football in Palmer Stadium. The game of football originated in 1869 as a contest between the College of New Jersey (Princeton) and Queens College (Rutgers). There were twenty-five players on each side and the game was more like soccer than the present-day football. Nevertheless, an important part of American lore had begun. There were two matches played that year, Rutgers winning the first, 6 goals to 4, and Princeton the second, 8 goals to 0. The first game was also marked by the first wrongway player in American football history—a Rutgers man (never identified in the news accounts) who in his ardor forgot which way he was kicking and scored for Princeton.

Before there was Monday night football, or Sunday pro-games, bowl games, television or even radio, if such a period can be imagined, the Ivy League football game was a *cause célèbre*. And the Princeton-Yale game of 1893, which played to a crowd of fifty thousand in New York, was one of the greatest football games of all time. Everyone in the city became aware of the occa-

sion and most took sides, much as in 1956 when the Dodgers and Yankees vied for the World Series. Shopkeepers decorated their windows with orange and black or blue and white, while the majority were rooting for colleges they had probably never seen. The final score was Princeton 6 goals to 0.

In 1922 Princeton's "team of destiny" went to Chicago to beat Alonzo Stagg's "big ten powerhouse" in what was the Super Bowl of its day. This was the first football game in history to be broadcast over radio. In 1914, Edgar Palmer, class of 1903, gave funds to build Princeton's own stadium. It has a capacity of forty-two thousand which can be increased to fifty-two thousand with wooden bleachers. Like Harvard's stadium, which was built in 1903, Princeton's followed the U-shape of the ancient Greek stadiums and permitted a 220-yard straightaway for track meets. Yale chose a style more characteristic of the Roman coliseum and the amphitheater at Pompeii.

President Maclean forbade the students to participate, chased some himself, and threatened to expel anyone caught—but no one paid much attention and no one ever left for participating.

A form of football was first played in 1844 on Cannon Green with the entire school participating: A-M on one side and N-Z on the other. At the first intercollegiate game with Rutgers in 1869 there were twenty-five on a side. In 1879 there were fifteen, and by the following year eleven. Princeton developed a style called "association football" and used it in 1873 against Yale in what has become the longest continuous rivalry in American football. Harvard played a version of rugby, and in 1875 Columbia, Harvard, Princeton, and Yale agreed on the rougher rugby-like game with a clash of flying wedges and other strategies sufficiently brutal to cause President Theodore Roosevelt to step into the mayhem in 1905 and suggest some restraints. New rules were agreed upon which permitted forward passes and other ways of moving the ball.

The football games received unparalleled attention by the turn of the century. The 1893 game against Yale is considered one of the greatest played, with fifty thousand fans watching it at Manhattan Field in New York. Without the advantage of television and other professional contests, New Yorkers turned out for the Princeton-Yale game, although many had scarcely any knowledge of the universities or the teams they represented. The games were usually played on Thanksgiving, preceded by a parade up Broadway with most of the undergraduates participating. One student wrote the following account:

> The climax comes on Thanksgiving day, when we go to New York for the Yale game. The college goes en masse, leaving a score of musty bookworms and a dozen of stranded unfortunates in sole possession. Every man wears his orange-and-black button, and the Freshmen celebrate the first opportunity to wear colors by a prodigious display of orange ribbons on their umbrellas, canes, and hats.
>
> Then the game! Thousands of people, gaily decorated coaches, a profusion of streamers, and a rattling fire of hostile cheers. A storm of applause announces the appearance of the teams. A little practice, and then the excitement rises to a pitch absolutely painful as the line-up is made and a dashing V opens the battle. How they play! We win, or else we don't. If we win, New York isn't large enough for us that night. Every man, woman, and child on Broadway seems to be wearing orange-and-black, the world was never so bright, the theatres are crowded with spectators more bent on celebrating than on seeing the play, and after midnight a tired and happy crowd boards the "Owl" for Princeton, telling each other over and over again how it was done. If we lose, things are different.

Baseball got underway when the first intercollegiate game was played against Williams in 1874. Yale subsequently became the major rival but the games were played on the respective campuses, not in New York. When the team was playing in New Haven, the scores were periodically sent over the wires to the Western Union office. This concentration of the information flow allowed for occasional false reports. One student would go upstairs to the telegraph office and then suddenly dash down in wild excitement. His abbetors at the door would raise a cheer that was echoed over the entire campus—Princeton had won! The results however were not always consistent with these reports.

In 1874 Princeton rowed in its first intercollegiate regatta at Saratoga, in spite of the objections of Amherst that "you have to draw the line somewhere." This crew is credited with being the first Princeton organization to wear the orange-and-black colors. While intercollegiate sports were deemphasized by Woodrow Wilson they resumed momentum under John Hibben, who saw to the construction of Palmer Stadium and Baker Rink. Athletics were raised to a height of popularity because of their competitive nature. Intercollegiate rivalry on a field far surpassed intellectual contests. Academic competitions could not be measured conclusively; superiority was not always precisely measured. But on the field, a score was a score.

Beyond football, baseball, basketball and other athletic contests came a rush of extra-curricular activities. These swept in to fill the vacuum when the inner unity of the old classical college was lost in the diversified university. The Triangle Club, the *Daily Princetonian* and *Tiger* Magazine were all under full heads of steam by the turn of the century. Other activities followed and today the university offers a wide range of athletic and extra-curricular pursuits to capture the energy that would otherwise be spent on less productive activities. Today practically every sport receives official recognition, with the important condition that the individual must first and primarily be a student. And it was with this important precept that Princeton has let football slip from overall importance on campus. The seed was first sown in 1934 when Princeton declined to play Stanford in the Rose Bowl. This general agreement between Princeton and her Ivy Leage rivals was reached in 1954: that every athlete must be a fully qualified member of the student body and no special athletic scholarships were to be offered. Football players in the Ivy League graduate at a rate of 95 per cent of those admitted whereas nationally only about 30 per cent of college football players earn a degree. This makes Princeton's accomplishments today on the fields, the diamonds, or courts all the more remarkable.

To the victors, the spoils. This bonfire on Cannon Green celebrates Princeton's first unshared "big three" championship since 1966.

For many years Cannon Green was the site of undergraduate games such as quoits, prison base, and football. In the latter game, a type of glorified soccer, the entire college lined up, A to M versus N to Z. Since the 1890s, Cannon Green has been the focus of bonfires for championship football seasons, when they occur, and seniors' class day exercises.

The Fountain of Freedom in the reflecting pool of the
Woodrow Wilson School, designed by James Fitzgerald
and installed in 1966. Seven hundred gallons are
sprayed out every minute.

McCarter Theatre. This was a gift in 1929 of the Princeton University Triangle Club and of Thomas McCarter, class of 1888. For many years it has been used for pre-Broadway tryouts of new plays and post-Broadway tours of established hits. Both *Our Town* and *Bus Stop* are among successful productions that had world premieres here. It is hard to name an American stage star of the 1930s and 1940s who did not play McCarter—the Barrymores, Helen Hayes, Cornelia Otis Skinner, Katherine Hepburn, the Lunts...

In 1950, the Triangle Club gave McCarter to the university and since then a varied program of repertory productions, guest performances, dance, music, drama and film has offered the Princeton community a wide variety of cultural activities. The theater underwent an extensive renovation and expansion in 1985 and 1986.

A performance by the Princeton Triangle Club. Organized by Booth Tarkington, class of 1893, Triangle has had a tradition of undergraduate musical extravaganzas that at times became nationally famous. F. Scott Fitzgerald wrote lyrics for the shows and performed in several of them as an undergraduate. During the 1930s aspiring actors were attracted to Princeton in part because of the extremely popular Triangle Club, including James Stewart, José Ferrer, and Joshua Logan.

247

During the 1950s and 1960s the Triangle shows appeared frequently on national television (the Ed Sullivan Show for example) and continued extensive road tours long after the drama groups at other universities had begun to cut back. In 1963, Triangle returned to play two performances on Broadway after an absence of many years and organized its last rail tour with its own cars, playing fourteen cities during the Christmas holidays.

In 1971 a special performance was held by returning alumni in honor of Benjamin Franklin Bunn, class of 1907, who had been the Triangle Club's graduate treasurer for almost sixty years and who had died at the age of ninety-six. Uncle Ben, as he was known, was a great inspiration to all who were connected with Triangle. He was patient, polite, astute, and completely indefatigable, touring by rail or bus with every company until he was ninety. He would have continued except that he felt it was important for others to have a chance at the fun and challenge of leading a group of fifty young actors, musicians, stage hands, and business staff on a whirlwind tour during the year-end holidays.

The Triangle Club, smiling like a basketful of cats, lives on as though it had nine-times-nine lives. It is the Great Vitrine for youth, the Bulletin Board for young ideas, the proving ground for talent that still is permitted to fumble; it is a place to sing, to do pratfalls, to thumb one's nose at authority, to test the last liberties of adolescence, to taste the true wine of being an American.

—Joshua Logan, class of 1931,
from the foreword to The Long Kickline
by Donald Marsden, class of 1964

249

Opposite: Off to graduation on a foggy day—father and son at the journey's end.

Princeton is internationally known for its contributions to knowledge and basic research. But even more important, to my mind, are the values and attitudes we learned at Princeton: the importance of individual initiative and doing our very best in pursuit of whatever goals we set for ourselves, and the obligation to go beyond those goals and to be of service to our communities and to the nation.

—James A. Baker III, class of 1952, United States Secretary of the Treasury

Above: On Baccalaureate Sunday, the famous procession of trustees and faculty begins on the steps of Nassau Hall. A silver mace is removed from its case in the Prayer Room and carried at the head of the procession before the president of the university. It was given in 1956 by the citizens of the town on the two-hundredth anniversary of the opening of Nassau Hall, symbolizing the cordial and mutually beneficial relations between the town and the university.

Above: The Baccalaureate Service, held in the University Chapel, begins with the academic procession. It takes place on the Sunday preceding commencement. *Opposite*: The chapel is filled to its eighteen hundred seat capacity with additional standees in its two balconies.

Maturity at Princeton means learning to get along and work with others, including some older and wiser than oneself; learning to interact with others as well as to act alone; to acknowledge and embrace interdependence. That kind of maturity is very much enhanced by the way students and professors interact at Princeton.

—*Eugene Y. Lowe, Jr., class of 1971, Dean of Students*

These young girls have found the best way to go back to Nassau Hall, on the back of a tiger. Alumni may lead the way but the whole family joins in, sometimes with three and four generations.

Reunions

Going back, going back
Going back to Nassau Hall.
Going back, going back,
To the best old place of all.
Going back, going back,
From all this earthly ball,
We'll clear the track as we go back,
Going back to Nassau Hall.

These words by Kenneth Clark have been etched on the hearts of Princetonians for generations. In fact a friend of mine whose father and grandfather were Princetonians and Presbyterian ministers, and whose four brothers went to Princeton with him, once said that his earliest childhood memories are of singing two songs: "Jesus Loves Me" and "Going Back to Nassau Hall." For many years the College of New Jersey was simply referred to as Nassau Hall. It was a simple statement, then as it is now, that at the beginning of June one was going back to Nassau Hall. This could never be interpreted as anything other than returning to a Princeton reunion. Over the years more people go back to Nassau Hall than simply go. It is a phenomenon unique in the American college system—possibly unique in the world. The percentage and numbers are high by any standard, especially for a place that is neither easy nor particularly enjoyable for many at the time of their undergraduate trials.

No other university in the country has more loyal, affectionate, and generous alumni than Princeton. It is expressed in the form of gifts and in attendance at reunions. Princeton, unlike Harvard, Yale, and Stanford, has had no benefactors of enormous size. The endowment and buildings have been the result of many small and a few substantial gifts. With the completion of its $410 million Campaign for Princeton, her endowment stands at $1.9 billion, third largest in the country after Harvard and the University of Texas but significantly larger on a per capita basis.

The alumni have played a critical role in Princeton's history ever since 1826. The Alumni Association of Nassau Hall was formed by John Maclean to raise financial support when the college was at its nadir having separated from the Presbyterian seminary (its mother church). The Graduate Council was formed in 1909, replacing the earlier Committee of Fifty which had secured funds to finance the preceptorial system. Many of the buildings on campus have been named in honor of alumni who have generously contributed to the university.

Every year a sociological phenomenon occurs that defies stringent analysis. It is called Reunion Weekend, culminating in the P-Rade, with ten to twelve thousand alumni and their spouses and families dressed in orange and black costumes wending their way from Nassau Hall to the playing fields. The old guard walk or ride, as the case may be, after the twenty-fifth reunion class, followed by each succeeding class.

The weekend of reminiscing, marching, singing, and carousing is basic ritual—the affirmation of the bond between alumni and their college, an annual festival of initiation and rededication.

Unlike schools that tie reunions to commencement, Princeton keeps reunions separate. The old grads don't have to share the spotlight with anyone else. They take over the campus and most of the town, and the resulting weekend is better experienced than described.

Above: Members of the classes of 1913 and 1969 at reunions, fifty-six years apart. When the first was at Princeton radios had not yet been invented. When the other came, there was a man on the moon. Both have Princeton in common.

Opposite: Roommates from the class of 1912 back for their seventieth reunion at the age of ninety-two. Who needs a cane when a friend's arm will do?

A Princeton prayer: *Dear Lord, make me a sophomore again . . . just for tonight. Amen.*

Norman Thomas, class of 1905, clergyman and perennial socialist candidate for president, who never missed a reunion, once said, "Some things in life justify themselves emotionally without necessity for analytic reasoning. On the whole, Princeton reunions fall in that category."

Opposite, top: Many of the wives have become so closely identified with their husbands' classes that they eventually carry on alone.

Opposite, below: An Alumni Council gathering at reunions. This organization traces its antecedents to 1904 and has been providing leadership for alumni activities for over eighty years. Its membership of about 280 includes presidents of alumni classes and regional alumni associations.

Above and opposite: Members of the class of 1941 celebrating at a class cocktail party in the north court of the graduate college's Procter Quadrangle.

Before and after the P-Rade. This annual parade of alumni has become quite an unusual event with ten to fifteen thousand participants and as many as thirty bands punctuating the long procession. Classes have major gatherings every five years and members make special efforts to attend these. Woodrow Wilson came up from the White House in 1914 to attend his thirty-fifth but for his fortieth in 1919 he cabled his regrets because he was in Paris for the Peace Conference. More distant duties kept astronaut Charles Conrad away from his twentieth in 1973. He sent word to his reunion chairman that "he was out of town on business." The message came from Skylab I, the country's first space station, to the Johnson Space Center in Houston, which relayed it to Princeton.

The P-Rade, led by the university band and the twenty-fifth reunion class, wends its way from the front campus, around Cannon Green, along McCosh Walk and on to the playing fields. The tradition began soon after the Civil War, and gradually the classes began to distinguish themselves by using class hats, blazers, balloons, and parasols. In 1907, the class of 1897 dressed as Dutch boys made an arresting sight and sound as they clattered along in their wooden shoes. In 1910, a class paraded in long gowns as suffragettes. Over the years alumni have appeared as Mexican bull fighters, Roman gladiators, convicts, Apache dancers, Confederate soldiers, the French Foreign Legion, Japanese Samurai, African hunters, firemen, chefs, baseball players, spacemen, and of course, tigers. Only once in over one hundred years has the P-Rade been cancelled due to weather (although many times progress in the rain has been challenging) and this was in 1953 due to a hurricane.

Opposite and left: 1932 and 1917 marching by as 1983 (*above*) reviews and waits its turn. Members of 1983 are wearing the traditional tan beer jackets, which trace their origins to the class of 1912, who donned denim coats and coveralls during their drinking socials at the Nassau Tavern. White jackets were first used by the entire class of 1913 and class insignia were first used by the class of 1920. One of the most famous designs was the once-in-a-century opportunity exploited in the mid-1960s—a black ball marked with $\sqrt{64}$.

Tune every heart and every voice,
Bid every care withdraw;
Let all with one accord rejoice
In praise of old Nassau.
In praise of old Nassau, my boys,
Hurrah! Hurrah! Hurrah!
Her sons will give, while they shall live,
Three cheers . . . [you know the rest]

Index

Italicized page numbers refer to illustrated material.